A CUP OF COMFORT®
for Writers

Inspirational stories
that celebrate
the literary life

Edited by Colleen Sell

adamsmedia
Avon, Massachusetts

*For Mom, the poet, for inspiring and encouraging
my love of language and literature*

Material on page 119 is from the book *Ghost in the Garden*, Copyright © 2005
by Beth Kephart. Photographs Copyright © 2005 by William Suit. Reprinted
with permission of New World Library, Novato, CA. *www.newworldlibrary.com.*

A Cup of Comfort® is a registered trademark of F+W Publications, Inc.

Published by
Adams Media, an F+W Publications Company
57 Littlefield Street, Avon, MA 02322. U.S.A.
www.adamsmedia.com and *www.cupofcomfort.com*

ISBN 10: 1-59869-268-2
ISBN 13: 978-1-59869-268-6

Printed in the United States of America.

J I H G F E D C B A

Library of Congress Cataloging-in-Publication Data
A cup of comfort for writers / edited by Colleen Sell.
    p.   cm. — (A cup of comfort book)
        ISBN-13: 978-1-59869-268-6 (pbk.)
        ISBN-10: 1-59869-268-2 (pbk.)
    1. Authorship—Anecdotes. I. Sell, Colleen.
        PN165.C87 2007
        808'.02—dc22
        2007017701

*This book is available at quantity discounts for bulk purchases.
For information, please call 1-800-289-0963.*

Contents

Acknowledgments

Producing an anthology, such as this, that combines the distinctive voices of numerous authors into a cohesive whole requires collaborative effort. So I have a great many people to acknowledge—foremost, the talented writers whose stories grace these pages.

I am most grateful to the superior staff of Adams Media, particularly Laura Daly, Meredith O'Hayre, Kate Petrella, and Jennifer Oliveira.

My heartfelt appreciation goes to the Scribe Tribe, my band of merry writer pals, for their encouragement, inspiration, guidance, love, and pure fun.

Every writer should be so blessed as to have the support that I unfailingly receive from my family, most especially my husband, Nikk—even though he doesn't "get" the writing shtick any more than I get his passion for all things motorized.

Introduction

"I shall live badly if I do not write, and I shall write badly if I do not live."

~Françoise Sagan

Like most writers, I did not become a writer. I simply am a writer. Always have been, always will be. I write because I cannot not write. And when I go too long with too little writing, I feel off, out of sorts, surly, and anxious and sad. Yet, even when I do not record them, even when I stifle them and shoo them away—Not now, I'm too tired, too busy, too distracted with work, with life—the stories come, refusing to be shushed. And eventually, I listen; I let the words, the stories out; I write. I must.

Still, it took a while for me to realize that writing is not just something I do; it is an essential part of who I am. It took even longer to reconcile my writing life with the rest of my life. How can I be a writer *and* a wife, mother, grandmother, daughter, granddaughter, sister, aunt, in-law, friend, employee, businesswoman, housekeeper, gardener, dancer, hiker, singer, activist? I often wondered. Sometimes, it did not seem possible. Sometimes, it seemed I would have to choose: writing or a "normal" life. Sometimes, I felt like an alien in my own life. . . . Until I connected with other writers. Until I found my tribe.

What I found, through my communion with other writers, is that the writer's life is about living and writing. It's not either/or. It's not even about striking a balance between writing and living. It's about combining writing with living in order to be whole. Of course, that is easier said than done. That's why we, the odd assortment of writers who make up the venerable tribe of storytellers, must help one another find and sustain that holistic equilibrium.

Writers get writers. And not many other people do. So it is important, I believe, for us writers to share our experiences and emotions, to tell of our trials and our triumphs, and to speak our truths about the writing life. On the pages that follow, more than fifty writers share their personal stories about what it is to be, and what it means to be, a writer. Their testimonials remind me of a remark by Bernard Malamud, who, when he was asked what writing had meant to him, said, "I'd be too moved to say." I am moved by the stories in A Cup of Comfort® for Writers. I trust you will be too.

~Colleen Sell

Hummingbird's Journey

Years ago, in the midst of dreaming of becoming a writer, seeing the shadow of my future writer-self outside my window, I entered a crisis.

An identity crisis.

A breakdown.

A depression.

A block.

There are many names in our culture for such experiences. Sometimes they come after a life change—a death, a divorce, a move. Sometimes they sneak up on us—we are driving merrily down our lane, and suddenly we see a stop sign from God.

Sometimes we stop. Other times we don't, and then we get hit by oncoming traffic.

This was my stop sign: I was walking around my yard one fall morning, filling the bird feeders, and I thought, "When I die, I don't want to have lived my life as only a professor." A vision of my life stretched out before me: standing year after year in a windowless classroom with desks bolted to the floor in neat rows. I had been teaching at a small women's college in the southeast, but like Georgia O'Keeffe, who taught there before me, I wanted more than that. I wanted to be a writer. I had dreamt of becoming a writer ever since childhood, and it was time, I decided, to make that dream come true.

At that moment, a hummingbird whizzed by me in the backyard, brushed past my shoulder, then stopped in mid-flight right in front of me, and looked at me. She chirped. I had begun the hummingbird's journey.

I obeyed the stop sign, slowly. I did not run that day. I waited, responsibly, teaching dutifully until the end of the semester, and then I quit my job, and after the winter holidays, I left. I left my husband and stepdaughter to go to a two-week-long writers' workshop in Mexico.

My teacher at the workshop was Pat Mora, a Chicana poet and storyteller. She was kind and grandmotherly, but in a sexy, laughing kind of way. On our first weekend in Mexico City, she led a group of students through the night streets of a festival, telling us about her childhood memories of El Paso and the Mayan, Spanish, and Catholic traditions that live on throughout eleven of the United States that only as recently as 1848 were part of the Mexican nation. I knew many of the facts of the history, but here it was, alive.

I'd sent samples of my poetry for her to read and evaluate ahead of time, and I desperately wanted her to like me. On the first night in our mountaintop hotel in Central Mexico, we sat together on a chocolate-brown couch in a large room with high wooden-beamed ceilings, and she said to me, "If you spent as much time and effort on your poems as you have on your academic work, you could be a success."

I took it as an insult.

Poetry was about inspiration, I thought. Not work. It had more to do with mood and magic than research and revision, I thought.

I was wrong.

One afternoon near the end of the two-week workshop, I paid a local taxi driver to take me away. I wanted to go deeper into the forest—escape the mountaintop hotel and the students' daily competition and nightly drinking and the small, nearby village with its American tourists circling for pottery and silver, cheap.

We drove south for hours, up and down and into the landscape. The taxi driver's radio was on, and from time to time the Latin disco music would be interrupted by male American voices, DEA or CIA agents on planes, reporting back to base. We were not far from Chiapas.

Finally the driver stopped.

"*Claro, vamos pués,*" he said, getting out of the car.

I hesitated.

"*Es lindo aqui. Vien.*" It's pretty here. Come on.

I followed him, nervously. I was in the middle of nowhere. Anything could happen. But then, I told myself, that was true anywhere. I'd probably be in more danger in downtown Manhattan.

I thought about the Virgin of the Mountains regalo that hung from the taxi driver's rearview window, and what he'd told me about his daughters, and how he said his wife's *pollo con molé* was like poetry. Like heaven.

"*Como poesía, como cielo,*" he'd said. "*Lo que es si bueno que todo es paz en su corazón.*" Like poetry, like heaven. Something so good that everything is peace in your heart.

That was what I was searching for.

That was the hummingbird's journey.

To peace in the heart.

We walked through the brown valley of a Mayan ruin, dry winter air caressing our faces. We were quiet. All of a sudden, we came upon the sound of a trickling stream, and there they were: dozens of hummingbirds with wings of turquoise, rose, and blue, the colors of the Mexican mountains at sunrise. I had arrived at the hummingbirds' winter place.

And in that place is found peace in the heart: being true to yourself, listening to your muses and using your own talents and following your own path, no matter how dusty, until you come upon your own water, your own food to get you through the winter, until the coming of spring.

Then comes another season in the life of the writer. There is growth enough in the garden, but no one comes to admire your colors, all you have begun to create and become.

This happened to me, a few years after the flight to Mexico. I had written many poems and essays, even had three books completed and had started submitting them for publication. But month after month, rejection after rejection came.

My writer friend, Greg, told me to think of publishing as a boomerang—just keep sending it away, and if it comes back, send it out again.

The problem was that one summer so many boomerangs came back that, before I could catch them, they hit me in the head.

So I took off, again. This time I piled my manuscripts

into the trunk of my little Geo Metro and flew west across the continent upon its red wings.

I rushed through the swamps of Georgia, Alabama, and Louisiana, and landed on the plains of Central Texas, where I finally took Pat Mora's advice. I did original, archival research in Austin that would eventually lead to the publication of one of the manuscripts I carried. I followed the course of the Rio Grande, from its green bottom to its cactus mountain tips, visiting the homelands of some of my favorite Mexican American and Native American writers. I drove further west, and I walked and I learned about this land and its people and history, what cannot be found in most books, and what, I would later discover, would bring new depth to both my writing and teaching.

In northern New Mexico, I stopped to change the oil—I'd logged over 3,000 miles—and then headed to Ojo Caliente to drink and bathe and get massaged in its famous mineral springs.

It was on my second day there that I met Elizabeth, a grand smiling woman writer from Colorado, another hummingbird on a journey.

I was doing yoga poses in the water, and she asked me about them. I could tell from her eyes that she wanted to talk. I told her about my cross-country mission, my flight from publication rejection, and my attempt to be who I was trying to become.

"Me, too," she said. "During the school year, I teach high school English, but every summer I come here to rest and re-gather, and then go home again."

"How do you do it?" I asked her. She was twenty years my senior and had managed to hold together a marriage, a family, a home, a job, and the mind of a writer.

"I come here," she answered. "It's good for me, and I return to my husband and son with a new appreciation. Then I take the summer to write, using all the ideas I've stored during the school year, so in the fall I can return to my students with renewed enthusiasm."

I nodded, slowly waving my arms in the warm water as I took in her words.

Later, dressed and dry in the parking lot as we said goodbye, I gave her a copy of one of my book manuscripts, with gratitude for the gift her story had given me, knowing that somehow I would make it—as a wife, mother, teacher, and writer. It was only a question of when.

It has been almost a decade since then. My stepdaughter will leave for college at the end of this summer, and my husband and I now have a lovely, six-year-old daughter too. I am still married. Still teaching. And I am, deep in my heart and on paper, a writer.

I have learned, on my hummingbird journeys, that my dreams about writing needed much more than inspiration or luck or the hope of a happy end.

I needed to discover how to balance hard work with the magic of language. How to push through each day with perseverance and discipline, and only occasionally give in to an outrageous urge or a whim. How to pay attention to my family and provide a steady, if small, income that nourishes us all daily. For in the end, I am human, not hummingbird, and I needed to learn how to integrate writing into my everyday life, not just get glimpses of it on cross-country journeys and fancies of flight with their potential dangers to life and limb.

Writers know well the energy that comes from these hummingbird journeys: the chance meeting that leads to opportunity, the block becoming breakthrough during a workshop, the long thoughts of the road that allow for a deeper understanding, or an idea for a project so profound that it puzzles us why we couldn't have seen it all along.

The problem, when we are first beginning, is how to make it through daily life. It helps to think of hummingbirds staying still. They may hover in one place, but in order to do so, they beat their wings seventy times per second, using all of the energy of their tiny hearts to stay afloat, looking out with their iridescent eyes for the nearest trumpet flower or butterfly bush, something to dip their delicate tongues into so they can suck out the sweet nectar that will sustain them.

It's hard work. Sometimes my heart beats as fast as a hummingbird's as I hurry and try to stay focused and balanced and healthy so I can fit it all in: my writing, my teaching, my family, my friends. For as much as those early journeys inspired me, at a time when I needed the adventure and vision that long-distance travel can give, I have learned that there are smaller journeys that must be made in order to achieve true success:

To the bench outside my bedroom window where I sit, and write, and wait for dawn. To the grocery store and the garden, so I can find food for my family, something healthy to keep us grounded and strong. To my daughter's school, where I volunteer to read stories and poetry about the fragile beauty of the earth. To the yoga studio, where I teach and take classes under the shade of a real tree, so I can slow down and breathe and get balanced. To the community college, where I teach students who barely made it through high school but still deserve the best education their small paychecks can afford. To my home, my heart, my husband, at the end of the day, where we laugh and talk and share stories of our daily journeys. To bed, where we love each other and provide a safe nest for ourselves and our daughters, so we can rest through the night and prepare for the next day. And to the land of dreams and prayers, where we remember we are part of something much greater than our solitary selves: this great world and her creator, who cares for us all, even the smallest hummingbird just beginning to make her own way.

~Cassie Premo Steele

Groupie

I've never been much of a joiner, but after getting cancer, I found myself weighing the benefits of two different groups: a cancer support group and a writing group.

Bladder, colon, breast, lung, prostate, leukemia, multiple myeloma, kidney. Chemotherapy, hair loss, nausea, mouth sores, pain, neuropathy. As we went around the conference-room table and people gave updates on their cancer and treatment, the words ricocheted off the walls and each one seemed to jab at me. How did I end up in a room with all of these sick people? Oh yeah. That's right. I'm in the Cancer Club now.

It was my turn. Everyone looked at me with encouraging eyes, as this was my first time at the meeting. "I have a rare form of pancreatic cancer called islet cell cancer." I immediately launched into my quick disclaimer, intended to make people feel better about my diagnosis. "It's not the bad kind where you're given six to twelve months to live; my oncologist says I could have seven years or more. My treatment is monthly injections, and I feel pretty well." Right then, though, my heart raced as though I'd just finished a 50-yard dash. Telling people that I had cancer still felt like a lie, like admitting to the worst kind of failure.

But I'd read that people who attend cancer support groups live longer than those who don't. I needed as many tricks in my bag as possible, so I'd decided to give it a try. I had a history of failed attempts at joining groups, but here I was. Twenty men and women, mostly in their sixties and older, were at the Tuesday morning Living with Cancer support group. They all seemed to know each other and in casual conversation referred to the meeting simply as "group." The term bugged me. Had I unwittingly become a groupie?

I felt like I had an open wound through which all my energy poured out as I listened to one after another describe their sicknesses and treatment in agonizing detail. My face must have shown my distress, because as I tried to slip out of the room after two excruciating hours, one of the cancer counselors caught up with me on my quick exodus to the elevator.

"Lori, I'm so glad you could make it this morning," she said.

"Well, thanks. I am too," I lied. I pushed the up button on the elevator.

"We recommend that you come at least three times before you decide whether or not it's a fit for you."

I was skeptical. But I did want to live longer, didn't I? "Okay," I said. "I'll see you next week."

Before the elevator had finished its short trip one floor up, images of my attempts to become a part of a group flashed through my mind like a slide show. There was my short-lived experiment with PAL softball the summer after fifth grade, when I discovered I didn't really like running and that I preferred reading to swinging a bat. Quitting the Girl Scouts in the sixth grade was an act of rebellion; my radio had been confiscated at a camp-out in the local high school gym. It wasn't that I was so into music at that time, but I was even less enamored with sleeping on a hard wooden floor. Then, in my junior year of high school, I tried out for and made letter girl, a second-tier cheerleader. It turned out I wasn't all that cheery and was ready to quit after football season, but my best friend, Tami, also a letter girl, talked me into staying through basketball season, thus finishing the year. Even though other groups would tempt me with their promises, from high school on I was a committed nonjoiner.

A couple of months before I went to my first cancer support group, I'd enrolled in a memoir-writing workshop. Both were on my list of things to do after I was diagnosed, quit working, and went on disability. I joined the support group because of the promise of a longer life, and the writing workshop because I'd harbored fantasies about being a writer. I also hoped writing would be a way to process some of my cancer-related angst.

The first class was terrifying. The instructor asked us—about eight women—to introduce ourselves and tell why we were in the class and what we were working on. *Holy cow!* I thought. *I can't drop the cancer bomb on a group of unsuspecting strangers.*

When my turn came, I said, "I've had some recent changes in my life, and I'm hoping that writing about them will be kind of like therapy." Not quite a lie, but a major detour around the truth. I felt my heart thump and looked to the next person to deliver me from everyone's attention.

That first session, a woman who was working on a book-length family memoir read a chapter. It grabbed me from the start; it was well written and featured a famous Hollywood couple as parent and stepparent. A fresh wave of insecurity washed over me. I glanced around to see how others were reacting. They all looked as if this story were no big deal, like they all had something equally unique up their collective sleeve. I had just left a twenty-year career in high-tech marketing, where confidence was my middle name. Now I felt like an insecure fourteen-year-old with bad acne.

After class, I waited until everyone left and approached the teacher. I had no idea who this person was, but because of her kind and constructive feedback during class, she seemed approachable. Ariel had dark, curly hair that contrasted in every way with my own cropped, string-straight, highlighted blonde hair. She wore slouchy bell-bottom jeans with a wide belt, flip-flops, and a tank top that revealed a couple of tattoos on her shoulders. She didn't look anything like the starched authority figures I was used to in business.

"I think I may be too much of a beginner for this class," I said. I detested my own lack of confidence.

"I think there are other beginners too," she assured me. "Why don't you try the assignment this week, and if you're still not sure next week, you can drop out."

I walked to my car and immediately called my husband, Steve, at work. "She wants us to write three pages of dialogue," I cried. "I don't have any idea how to write dialogue."

"Well, did you think it would be easy?" Steve asked. "Give it a try and see if you enjoy it."

Steve's a musician who practices almost daily. He makes it look effortless and somehow masks the dedication it takes. Was I motivated enough to apply that type of perseverance to writing?

I didn't quit. I started to enjoy the challenge and sense of purpose writing gave me. My confidence grew in the positive and supportive environment, and I became friendly with some of the other writers. I couldn't believe my luck at having landed in a group of such creative and smart women. The writing assignments turned long-forgotten childhood memories into full-fledged stories that deepened my love for my family. I remembered the wind in my hair on the many cable-car rides in San Francisco. The glug, glug, glug sound when my father poured water into a cup from a canteen as we drove across the Mojave Desert one summer to visit my great-aunt in Arizona. The smell of my grandmother's cinnamon rolls baking, while we kids sat at her kitchen eating fresh-picked blackberries swimming in cream.

The last assignment of the term was to write a 500-word story about grace. My mind immediately flew to the grace period I felt I'd been given when I was diagnosed with the good kind of pancreatic cancer—the kind where my life would be measured in years versus months. After knowing my writing group for two months, I felt that I owed them the truth of my situation. I sent Ariel an e-mail telling her I had terminal cancer, wanted to write about it, and did she think the group could handle it. She responded that she thought the group could and that she'd keep the discussion focused on the writing and not the content.

My mouth was dry that day when I read the piece in class, but as I finished up, no lightning bolts appeared to strike me down, and nobody died or even fainted. The silence was a bit longer than normal after I finished reading it, but Ariel quickly jumped in and directed the discussion to the writing. Afterward, a few people shared their shock with me and told me they were sorry. However, to my great relief, most of the conversation centered on everyone's writing. I did not feel singled out as a sick person—not one bit. I felt light, like I had wings, as if I couldn't be grounded by cancer.

I was ready to give the Living with Cancer support group a second chance. I sat down at the conference table and watched the room fill up with about fifteen people that day. The cancer counselor walked in, her arms burdened with heavy binders and clutching a votive candle in one hand. She sank into her chair, organized her papers on the table. She glanced at her watch, and at precisely ten o'clock she started group.

"The unfortunate reality of a group like this is that sometimes people die," she began. She invoked the name of the woman who'd died, and some people nodded as if already aware of her death. "Our tradition is to light a candle for the person, pass it around, and have everyone, if they wish, say something. I'll start."

She lit a match and put it to the candlewick, and the flame burst to life. Then she relayed a short story about the deceased and passed the candle to the next person. Each person in turn shared something about the woman who, I gathered from the comments, was the irreverent wife of a minister who hadn't been hesitant to use profanity when it came to discussing her ##&!!@# cancer. The flame danced in the air as one person slid it on the table to the next, and the vanilla fragrance floated in the air, comforting me like the aroma of baking bread. Then it was my turn. I felt the weight of everyone's words, of the woman's death, of my own cancer.

"I didn't know her, but I'm sorry for all of your loss," I stuttered. I passed the candle on quickly, afraid to hold death in my hands too long for fear it might singe me.

I left group that day more exhausted than I'd been the first time I'd attended. As I trudged out to the parking garage, I knew that my ghost of quitting groups was coming back to possess me. When I got home, I called the cancer counselor to tell her I was quitting.

"I leave the meeting feeling drained," I told her. "I'm in another group right now where I feel a tremendous amount of support."

"I understand," she said encouragingly.

As I placed the phone in its cradle, an immense weight lifted from my shoulders. Later that day I registered for the fall term of the writing workshop. I would fight cancer by joining a group of the living.

~Lori Maliszewski

Wasting Time

We're back from a three-week, 7,500-mile trek across America, my two sons and I. It has been one of those Experiences with a capital E, traversing the country on the diagonal, northwest to southeast and back, in a twenty-four-foot rented RV. My sons are thirteen and eleven, old enough to be decent company but young enough still to listen to me, at least some of the time. We saw what we planned to see: national parks, Civil War battlefields, historic settlements, the Mississippi, the Gulf, the Atlantic, their Orlando grandfather. But that's not what made the trip an Experience.

What made the trip an Experience was catching a glimpse of a pale green Luna moth with an eight-inch wingspan one night in Checotah, Oklahoma. And pulling into a gas station in Ogallala, Nebraska, just ahead of a pickup truck with an eight-foot statue of Elvis bungeed in the back. And the humid, buggy night we camped at Eskew's Landing, "Mississippi's Best Kept Secret," a 200-acre former plantation. "There's been an Eskew on this land since 1859," the old woman drawled from behind the counter.

I was there, but I came close to missing it. I was almost too busy being a writer.

For the first few days, as we barrel across Oregon, Idaho, Utah, and Arizona, my mind works overtime turning every observation into a story. My reporter's notebook is on the floor next to me, wedged between the driver's seat and a shoebox full of AAA maps. It couldn't be any closer unless it was on my lap.

Our second morning out, my older son falls asleep riding shotgun, and I sneak a glance at him: the long legs, the lanky arms, the feet that are suddenly two sizes larger than mine. By next summer he will have a deep voice. By next summer he will be giving me that sulky how-can-I-possibly-be-related-to-someone-as-lame-as-you look. I am sure there's an essay in this. I grab for my notebook, balance it on the steering wheel, and scribble ideas as we speed across southern Idaho.

Morning three, we drive through heavy fog west of Chicken Creek Reservation in central Utah. The weather looks ominous—gray and cold and stormy—and I steel myself for hours of tough driving. But the front I imagine turns out to be only a fog bank, and we are through it and back in sunshine in less than five minutes. I am so buoyed by this, by having something turn out so much better than I expected, that I want immediately to write about it: Hail the pessimist, who goes through life pleasantly surprised; pity the optimist, who can only be disappointed. I grab the notebook.

Day four, I fill pages with seventy-mile-an-hour scrawls. I am drowning in ideas: Everyone ought to love the place they live, reads one entry. I write it after watching a girl on horseback gallop across a field next to the highway. The land is baked brown and hard and dotted with scrub, unlovely and, I imagine, unloved. But the girl, her long, chestnut hair streaming behind her, has a huge grin on her face. She loves it.

Next page I write: "RV subculture—class collision," which comes from pulling into a KOA campground the night before and finding that our assigned space is between a $250,000 motor coach, featuring a washer and dryer and a 50-inch television, and a 1962 Airstream held together by duct tape.

Next page: Traveling west with Dennis and Phil in '71—when a trip was a trip. Then: The Zen of long-distance driving—meditation on the interstate. Finally: Planes, trains, and automobiles . . . how you get there matters. One of my pens is already running out of ink.

On day five, negotiating hairpin turns in Zion National Park, I am struck with an idea for another essay. I go for the notebook but realize I can't write and keep us on the road at the same time. "Zane," I call to my younger son, who has the best penmanship, "come up front and help me with something." I hand him the notebook and start dictating.

We inch around another switchback, the one-lane road snaking between towering cliffs the color of terra cotta. I keep talking and glance over at Zane to make sure he's getting it.

Then, I get it: There he is, head buried in a notebook, dutifully recording my words in his careful cursive so I can later make a tale out of a moment neither of us is living. Later that day, when we stop for gas, I take the notebook from its place by my seat and put it in an overhead storage cupboard next to a six-pack of SpaghettiOs.

Plato said, "the life which is unexamined is not worth living." But I don't think he meant examining should take the place of living. I don't think he meant we should be so busy mining our adventures for meaning that we don't have time to live them.

Of course, writers use their lives as text and context. That's part of the gig. Although I do not often write about myself, everything I have written in the past decade and a half is deeply connected to my life, a reflection of who I am or who I was or what mattered most to me. I know that life and art can mix, enriching both. But the danger—the danger I recognized when I saw my son hunched over a notebook instead of marveling at the landscape—is that art can overpower life. It can, for a long moment, actually replace the experience of living.

I recently met a woman whose mother had just died of cancer. She might have spent the last year of her mother's life with her mother, but instead she chose to spend it hundreds of miles away at the keyboard, crafting long, lyrical, literary letters about her mother's illness that she arranged to send to an acquaintance. Before she drafted the first letter, she imagined the book the letters would someday become.

She told me this proudly while on tour promoting the book, and I tried hard not to look horrified. I appreciate that writing can be therapeutic. No doubt the letters helped her through a difficult time. But writing also detached her from the present—from being present—and shielded her from the moment. Her present was painful, mine was pleasant, but we were both prisoners of our craft.

I was at first concerned, scared really, that I'd be wasting the experience of the trip if I didn't write about it. But I am beginning to understand that it pays to "waste" some things, if wasting means living the moment fully rather than taking notes on it for later.

We've been home for a while now, but I still cherish the long mid-June days I wasted with my sons, the mornings full of talk and silence, me driving, the boys taking their turns sitting up front by my side, sometimes dreamy, wordless, other times deep in monologues full of mind-numbing details about computer games and wars waged with little pewter action figures. But there was thoughtful talk too, conversations about what makes a good friend and how you decide what you want to be when you grow up and why grandma died.

At noon we would stop at some local park, where the boys would explore the terrain and play tag and fight off the insects, while I busied myself in the tiny kitchen heating up cans of Chef Boyardee ravioli and slicing apples. I loved to watch them from the window and listen to their voices, loud and confident. Wherever we were—Little America, Wyoming; Cape Girardeau, Missouri; Byhallyah, Alabama—they were immediately at home. The afternoon stretched out before us. We would eat and then spread the maps on the grass and plot the rest of the day: how many miles, how many states, which campground.

After lunch, they would often disappear into the

upper bunk for hours to drowse or read or play with their video games or get on each other's nerves. I drove in silence, happy to be close but separate. Some afternoons Zane would sit by my side, and we'd listen to a tape of *Wind in the Willows*, enjoying the tale as if we hadn't heard it a dozen times before, looking over and smiling at each other at the same silly bits of dialogue. Other afternoons it would be Jackson, my older son, who would join me. Sometimes we talked. Once we whiled away an afternoon composing an epic poem about roadkill. But often we simply sat together, our minds blanked by the tedium of the road. We listened to the thrum of tires on pavement. Time slowed.

There was real pleasure in that boredom, those hours and days and weeks of traveling together, of being together, of just being. The things we did, the places we saw, the thoughts we had about ourselves and each other were part of that time, and that time alone.

I think some adventures should be lived just for the sake of the adventure. Some feelings should be private; some lessons learned for one's benefit alone. Life, even for a writer, can just be life, not a narrative to be crafted and sold.

We leave for a camping trip to the mountains next week. The reporter's notebook stays at home.

~*Lauren Kessler*

Why Write?

Some questions do not lend themselves to easy answers. "Why do you love him or her?" "How can you tolerate that?" "What are you doing in there?" and "Have you been drinking?" are examples of queries that make us stop and stare, our mouths hanging open. My favorite responses to these types of personal probes are, "Because!" "Nothing!" and "No!" This proves that the training of my adolescence was not a complete waste of time.

Recently, a close friend asked me why I write. Because he, too, is a writer, I assumed the question was rhetorical. After a few seconds of silence I realized he was serious and expected me to cough up an answer. Quickly reaching into my memory bank and rushing through the file marked "No-Fault Responses," I blurted out, "Because!"

He was not impressed.

Why write? If "Because!" is not a suitable answer (which it obviously isn't), then why? Having learned the danger of answering for anyone but myself, I will attempt here to give a reasonably coherent explanation of why I put myself through the scary, frustrating, exhilarating ordeal of regularly eviscerating myself on paper for all the world to see.

This is my cue to begin with the tale of my unhappy childhood, the demons that drove me, and my frenzied escape into Fantasyland. Not only is that shamefully convenient, it is untrue. Yes, my childhood was unhappy. Yes, I had demons. Yes, I escaped into Fantasyland. However, I could just as easily have become a serial killer, a prostitute, a child beater, or a politician. God, in His infinite mercy, spared me, and I instead became a writer. I do not write because of my warped past; I write in spite of it. It gives me grist for the mill, but it is never anything more than grist. My passion, alone, keeps the wheel turning.

Young girls often fall in love with horses and festoon the tops of dressers and desks with the miniature likenesses of golden palominos, black stallions, or spotted appaloosas. I loved words with the same dreamy, irrational passion. The surface of every piece of furniture I owned was crowded with books and notebooks filled with my own scrawled creations.

I told stories to my sisters and wrote poetry for

my grandparents. My mother would ask me to read my latest adventure to her while she soaked in a hot tub at the end of a day that had been too long. I'd sit cross-legged on the bathroom floor, my notebook in my lap, and read. Every now and again, I'd glance up at my mother, her naked shoulders resting against the back of the tub, her eyes closed. Sometimes she looked dead, and I would stop, hold my breath, and wait. Then, her sleepy voice breaking the silence, she'd say, "'The fairies made a boat of old pine needles.' Go on."

My mother was my first critic. However, as we all know, mothers make lousy critics. If I'd read Dostoevsky to her for forty minutes, she would have proclaimed it "Wonderful!" and "Exciting!" Anyone who has ever read Dostoevsky needs no further explanation.

I write because I need to write. I write because I am at the bottom of a deep well and I am trying to tell you something. I am trying to make you hear me, to be heard. I am trying to get your attention, because there is this flame inside me and I am trying to tell you about it. I want you to know the fire I feel and the hunger that eats at me.

I write because I am standing at an intersection in my life and in your life and, while you hurry past, I am recording the world around both of us. I am taking note of everything, and I want to hold it up to you, mirrorlike, so you can see what I see.

I write because there are screaming things in my head, and they will not be still unless I am a witness for them, unless I tap the microphone at the top of the world, lean forward, and say, "The intensity of all that you feel cuts right through me; I feel it too. Being human is a glorious, hideous business! You are more magnificent than you ever hoped and more horrible than you ever feared!"

I write because, if I don't, I will explode. I will start banging my head against the floor and, when the night comes, I will do a Goya and paint monsters on my walls. I write because the words pack themselves so tightly inside my head—with all their energy, dread, joy, hope, and abject misery—that if I cannot get them out, they will consume me.

I write because I have something to say . . . about me, about you, about being alive.

I know you are thinking that I, like so many writers, must be just the tiniest bit insane. Well, I am grateful to God for many things, but chief among them is the fact that Annie Dillard exists. I have read of her childhood (penned by her own hand) and the remarkable fullness of joy it contained. I am thus reassured that not every writer is a mental cripple, born in despair, reared in anguish, and constantly fighting back the relentless tide of an impending full-blown nervous breakdown. I read Annie Dillard's work and say to myself, "See? She is brilliant and normal. It can be done!"

Thank God for Annie. If she can be a writer and be sane, maybe I can too.

I write because I am a writer. I was born that way. I was also born with brown eyes. What is one to do? You play the hand you are dealt. When I think of a painter, I see someone watching the colors and shades of the world and putting them to canvas. When I think of a musician, I see someone listening hard to the rhythm of the human heart and wrapping it in melody. When I think of a writer, I see someone on his hands and knees, leaning over the spilled blood of his soul, pooling in the dirt like the blood of Abel, and hearing his lifeblood, his lifework, cry out to God, "Here is my story! Here is my truth! Someone bear witness of me!"

I write because I love to write.

Why write? Because.

~Camille Moffatt

To Begin

This is how it is with me. . . .

Upon awakening, I arise, shuffle to the kitchen for coffee, and before the brew has completed its circulation—dripping, gurgling, the aroma filling my little log house set on a mountain in western North Carolina—I think, *Why did I write that sentence as I did? I must go back and change it. It doesn't work.* For while I slept, my brain did its own circulation, gurgling, dripping, brewing, and somehow, without any awareness of my cognitive, active, living brain as I slept, there came an awareness all the same, that something is Not Quite Right, and the action of arising joggled the idea of Wrong to the forefront, a first thought. However, I have things to do first, and so I tell myself that the Wrong must wait, but while it pretends, at first, to agree to waiting, it won't leave me alone. The Wrong nags and wheedles and cajoles, until I have to drop everything and fix what needs fixing. Open up Microsoft Word, change, rearrange, make perfect, save it to the file, and then I can carry on.

Back upstairs, I pour Deep Creek Blend into a thick pottery mug, watch the steam rise like a tiny ghost, watch it lift lighter than the air around it, tempting me with its ethereal cloud, its awakening smell. I take the first sip, always the best, and while drinking my coffee, I think, *I wonder who has read my work while I slept? I wonder if anyone has read the short story that was published? I wonder if anyone has read any of my essays? My poetry? My blog post? My Web site? My heart? My soul?*

Before the second cup has its first sip, I totter downstairs again, open up various pages, look to see whether anyone has left a comment, or perhaps I wonder if I will feel the essence of someone, some whiff of their interest left behind as a kind of indistinct and ephemeral fingerprint. I finish off my coffee, and try not to care so much whether someone has shown any interest in my writing. I pretend I matter to no one but myself.

Upstairs, I hear my husband, who I've affectionately named Good Man Roger, call down to me, "Are you coming for a walk with us?" Us, meaning our two dogs, Kayla and Jake, who also have found nicknames from me, Fat Dog and Not Quite Fat Dog.

I holler up to him, "Yes, just a moment. I'll be there. Hold on." And tear myself away from the computer Other times I am silent. Then, what must he think? For there is no schedule to my insanity or sanity. I am unexpected, I suppose.

Shashink shashunk goes the camera lens that is my brain. *Snap snap snap snap* goes the shutter of my creative thought, capturing images. There, an old man helping another old man to rise, and off they tottle. There, the perfect oval of a face in a side mirror. There, a young woman walks by, her raspy deep 1940s movie voice wishing a "good eve-ning." Wait! . . . interruption. . . . Good Man calling down to me, "Biscuits are done." And I call back, "I'm writing something." And he calls again, "They're hot!" And I think, *Wait wait wait, the thoughts are coming, wait.* And know I must go eat the biscuits while hot.

Up the stairs I climb, words trailing out behind me as dust motes, spilling out behind me as air currents, words falling out of my head, surrounding, swirling about me, onto the stairs and floor. Into the kitchen I go, the words messy around my feet from their falling about; I kick them away, pick some of them up and put them in my pockets for later, some I grab up and swallow, some enter my ears and huddle in my brain, some stick to my clothing. And I pick up a biscuit and put a piece halfway in and halfway out of my mouth, and to Good Man, I say, "Nywaw nywaw nuyah," making the biscuit piece flap on my lips so that Good Man laughs at me. I swallow the piece and say, "I was writing something." And he says, "Oh, good, is it something new?" and I say, "No, nothing new, just stuff, nothing new, just words, nothing new, just letters falling from my brain and spewing out of my fingertips, nothing new, just the chaotic ramblings of an unknown writer." And he smiles and butters his biscuit, and I smile crooked while I smear honey butter on mine. And I eat, fast, I stuff the biscuits and turkey bacon in my mouth, stuff and swallow fast, faster, washing it down with orange juice, I clean my plate in mere minutes, wash up the dishes for Good Man, since he cooked for me, fast, faster, and at last, I race back down to my computer, and already, my mind has moved on from the original thoughts. . . .

Where was I?

~*Kathryn Magendie*

The Zen of Rejection

Spring has finally arrived in our postage-stamp
yard. The twenty-foot walk to the mailbox
leaves shallow footprints in the moist earth, where
pale yellows, striated greens, and rusty reds are ready
to pop, pushing themselves up, up, up. I am mindful
to step clear of succulent new growth, satisfied that
soon this modest plot of land will turn into a pretty
little potager garden, as it always does this time of
year.

In the mailbox, a rejection letter threatens to
spoil the lovely day. I crumple my most disappointing
literary heave-ho to date in my fist. I have just found
out that the prestigious prize for which my book was
a finalist, the golden ring that would have transformed me into a successful, highly paid author, has
gone to someone else. Once again, I am an aspiring
novelist—a middle-aged woman who quit a perfectly

good job as a nurse to take up a pen and to caretake a sixteenth of an acre of land.

The daffodils bob their heads demurely, reminding me that gentle acceptance is the way to peace and beauty. I scowl at the daffodils and their exhausted neighbors, paper whites and Soleil d'Or narcissus. The pushy, sickeningly sweet smell of hyacinth wafts in the soft moist air, irritating my nostrils. The coy tenderness of sweet pea and spinach annoy me. I rant at the lusty, persistent, straining, popping buds of forsythia and azalea. Their profane fecundity, the whole sucking muck and mire and swell of spring, are enough to make my skin crawl.

I have the urge to stick a pitch fork in the compost pile. In layers of wet rotting leaf mold. In manure. So HarperCollins doesn't want my manuscript after all? Perhaps the compost wants HarperCollins? The sheet of fibrous organic material balled in my hand was dispatched by an organization that calls itself "The Bellwether Prize, In Support of a Literature for Social Change." I assume their missive is biodegradable. A well-established, hard-working heap of natural waste can worm paper to pulp quicker than mugwort can overtake a perennial bed.

I soak the letter in the dregs of kitchen waste and leftover dishwater to aid in its decomposition. Then I grab the green plastic pail from its spot on the counter next to the sink. The bucket of slop swinging in my hand has a satisfying weight.

The dishwater, asparagus stems, egg shells, coffee grounds, and scrapings of red pepper pasta land on top of the layer of leaves and lime from my last excursion to the heap. I've used the same system for years: a layer of garbage, a layer of lime, a layer of yard waste, a layer of manure, if available, not necessarily in that order. Today, I add an extra layer to the recipe for reclaimed earth—one thin page of wet rejection between lime and cow dung.

I put my back into it, pitching my fork into the half-cooked pile on my left, turning it over on top of the new pile in front of me, sweating and straining with righteous purpose. A leathery orange rind almost makes me cry. I toss the dried-up peel on top of the mound. I get a rhythm going: stab, lift, pitch, stab, lift, pitch. After a half hour of thrusting, twisting, and tossing, I'm not burying my ego any more; I'm turning the compost heap. I notice that the warm breeze is drying my sweat almost as fast as I can produce it. I take off my sweatshirt and feel the sun on my arms. Hard as I try to avoid being taken in, I can't ignore the slant of light playing on the branches of the quince bush a few yards from the heap. Red blossoms against shiny green leaves scream, Look at me! I know this bush is too full of itself for its incarnation of a quince to last. But wouldn't I be a fool to let the moment pass unnoticed?

I haven't reached Nirvana. I'm not one with the universe. But I haven't embarrassed myself by writing an unwarranted nasty letter to an editor at Harper-Collins or bothered any of the well-published judges of The Bellwether Prize with a ridiculous whining phone call. The breeze has died down. The daffodils have stopped bobbing. Okay, I can live with the fact that their shaking heads were not a response to the bad mood I'd degenerated into because of a sheet of paper I'd found in my mailbox. I don't even care that this parallelism of writing and gardening—this creation, decay, and rejuvenation metaphor—might embarrass the sophisticated reader. My hands and butt ache pleasantly, and in a month the compost will be ripe enough to dress the kohlrabi and kale.

~Sally Bellerose

This story was first published in *Poets & Writers* magazine, November/December 2000.

Thomas Wolfe Wasn't Kidding

Y ou can't go home again."
     The words linger: "You can't go home again."
. . . Not if you write, and not if you have a family.

Somewhere between the fourth and fifth drafts of my first novel, *Dive*, I began attending a writing workshop. I had just sold the book, a coming-of-age story that my editor and I saw as a crossover title—one that would reach both teen and adult readers. Not being very clever, I agreed to read aloud my first night in class. That was the format: three or four people read up to fifteen pages; everyone listened; a discussion followed. Until then, my only audience had been my editor, hence the latest rewrite.

I read from a chapter in which Virginia, or V, my fifteen-year-old heroine, is looking back at an episode in her childhood. It's summer, and her family is driving to the beach. Occurring late in the book, it's a pivotal scene from which the book's title comes, in which V learns, at the hand of her father, a memorable lesson about life.

There's nothing quite like the silence of a room full of writers. They are much less like a hushed and anticipatory audience than a legion of hawks circling an unsuspecting songbird nest, and when they finally speak, you long for that silence again.

"My daughter is fifteen and she doesn't sound like that. V's voice is too old," John said.

"The writing is good, but I want details: How hot was it that day? Was the water rough or calm? What else was happening?" Betty said.

"When they're in the car, you bring up hard-boiled eggs. Then they just disappear. What happened to the eggs?" Harriet asked.

Did I hear someone say the writing was good? They dismantled the chapter—each scene, the sentences, the details. What happened to the eggs? I was hooked.

I made my way through the fifth draft, feeling alternately elated and suicidal. I'd get stuck and question everything, wonder how I'd ever find my way to the end. What had made me think I could write a book?

Fortunately, I had encouragement and guidance from my editor. And I was able to weigh her comments against those of the workshop participants. I also made a few discoveries. Among them was finding how hard it is not to believe that a patch of dialogue is dull or that a chapter is too long when someone says as much and twenty heads nod in unison. I found that no matter how many times the correct usages of lay/lie and I/me are patiently explained, I can't grasp them. "Me don't know what else to tell you," they said.

So in this room full of writers I learned how to laugh at my limitations as a writer, and later, more essentially, at myself. I didn't know it then, but learning to laugh would have everything to do with *Dive*.

In the book, one of several recurring images—initially brought to my attention by my editor—is of V's throat, in which words and feelings are constantly stuck. She is often swallowing truths, wherein new and painful realizations reside. She becomes aware that feelings, as they arise in her throat, find expression there. As V's creator, I had to ask myself everything the image meant and then use that meaning to its best effect.

Personally, the image began to embody the question of whether I, as a writer, was going to tell the truth. I would. Then, how much of the truth would I tell? How, too, would I answer other people's questions: "How much of it is true?" "What made you write the book?" "How is a book for adolescents different from a book for adults?"

How much truth would I tell? That answer was easy. All of it, because I was writing fiction and could thereby remain in the shadow of what was really real. All of it, because I really had experienced the loss of a father, the loss of a mother as she progressively left a sober reality for an alcoholic one, the experience of losing one friend and then finding another—astoundingly, to fall in love with.

What compelled me to write the book? That question was also simple to answer. The books that had gripped me as an early adolescent were *The Red Badge of Courage, Johnny Get Your Gun, Heart of Darkness, Crime and Punishment*—stories of battles, blood, despair. They say to write what you know. What did I know of crime? I'd never been to war, never committed a crime. I knew only the crimes of my family, the war of becoming myself. Card catalogs antedated computers, before which I'd stood in my pubescent angst, searching under A for alcoholism, under H for homosexual, under L for lesbian. I didn't find the catalog references; there were no books.

At fifteen, I knew that my parents drank more than other people's parents, were dangerous and unpredictable when they did. And I fell in love with the new girl in town. I wrote *Dive* in part because

I remembered myself at fifteen, losing a battle against my parents' drunken despair and being alone, with no words to guide me, in that dark reality. I also remembered the exquisite loneliness of falling in love with another girl, knowing by the thick silence surrounding that love that something about it was supposedly wrong.

So I wanted someone else—especially a teen who might be having a similar experience—to be able to find a book in the card catalog or computer under those subjects. By now, of course, there are many. Still more are needed.

The Library of Congress catalogs *Dive* as being about family life; brothers and sisters; friendship; death; lesbians; alcoholism; and dogs. Seeing "dogs" in that list has always made me smile. *Dive* is about a small black shadow of a dog. And about the shadows separating truth from fiction.

How much of the book is true? When I was a kid, we had a dog named Lucky. He was a little black mutt. In *Dive*, there's a little black mutt named Lucky. In the book, I created an explanation for his name by way of a memory in which V and her parents choose a dog at the local pound. Her father asks, "Which one?" and V points to the little black shadow in the corner. When they see the dog V has chosen, her mother announces that German shepherds are good watchdogs and that maybe they should get one of those. Accepting V's choice, her father laughs and says, "I'd say he was a pretty lucky dog." That's when V says, "Lucky, let's go, boy." Not only does the dog get named, but the conflict between mother and daughter is set in place. V recalls that moment, which occurred eight years prior to the time the story takes place, just after Lucky has been injured by a hit-and-run driver, which is how the book begins.

How much of that conflict between mother and daughter is real, and how much of fiction is really wish fulfillment? At first, I worried that the workshop would find the scene lacking in suspense, unbelievable, even melodramatic. They didn't. It was only me, worrying over the idea that what happens in life does not necessarily translate into lifelike fiction.

For it was just as true that there'd been a real dog named Lucky in my life and that he'd been run over one dewy morning in the suburbs when I was about eleven. It was just as true that I held the shaky little bundle in my arms in the car seat next to a stranger who'd witnessed the accident and was kind enough to drive us to the vet, because nobody else in my family was home. It was just as true that the vet and this stranger had waited while I spoke to my mother at work from the vet's phone, and that I began to choke back tears and my feet froze, and that the vet lifted the phone from my hand. But then fact and fiction diverge.

In the book, the vet said "around five hundred dollars," but in life he'd said three hundred. In the book, the vet tried to smile when he said Lucky was going to sleep. In life, he'd grimaced and wouldn't even look at me. I didn't really understand what was happening. The stranger tried to hug me, and I pushed him away. I was cold, hard as frozen ground. The vet's voice was sharp when he'd said, "Hold the dog." My hands were already rubbing Lucky's ears when the vet slid a large needle under Lucky's fur. I was numb. Three hundred dollars.

In *Dive*, V says, "She won't pay? Fine. I can pay, if you'll let me work for you." In life, I never said that. I was mute, numb, trauma personified, all of eleven. All I could do was stand there and watch my dog die.

Sometimes fiction is wish fulfillment. In *Dive*, Lucky lived. Yet without the incident in life, *Dive* would have been a different book. In the story, Lucky's convalescence is the means by which V steps away from her immediate experience and begins to observe and ultimately discover the sources of her mother's trauma. It's the moment that she begins to separate from the innocence of her own childhood and turn a maturing eye to her experience.

So can we hope that fiction sometimes acts as

a salve for the truth? At that moment, when fiction fulfilled a wish that reality had denied, I certainly did. Perhaps that's one reason so many of us are willing to climb the stairs to the workshop each week and bare some part of ourselves to each other with our words.

There's one question more: How is a book for teens different from one for adults? The adult in me muses over an answer, while my adolescent voice shouts, There is no difference! The adult is silent. I'm satisfied.

What happened when *Dive* was published was that my family stopped speaking to me. Each person had a different reason, but I felt it coming like a storm rising. They were scared. They had thought I might tell. And I did.

As hard as a chain is to break, it begs to be broken. There exists a genetic chain of alcoholism in my family. One of its rules is that nobody speaks about it, dares to tell the truth. In *Dive*, I told that truth, breaking the rule, breaking the chain of silence.

Having done so, I've discovered that there's a silence louder and sharper than the one death carries—the silence of the living. Years have passed since I've communicated with my family, been included in the connections, the information passed between relatives. Each week I leave that silence and climb the stairs to the workshop, where I hear other voices, other truths, being written and discussed. Sometimes I just close my eyes and listen. Friends in the workshop have no idea what they mean to me; sometimes there are no words.

The first draft of *Dive* was written long ago, but it was then that my father's only brother, John Donovan, himself a pioneer for having written the first novel for teenagers in which two boys fall in love, said to me, "You'll have to decide, when this book is published, how much it'll bother you when your family stops speaking to you."

I really didn't understand what he meant then. I do now. You can go home again, but only if you're willing to leave forever. What happened to the eggs? When I heard those words, I knew I'd found my new family.

~Stacey Donovan

The Day I Turned Scarlett

It had to be 100 degrees in my dorm room that night, and by two o'clock in the morning, I was hot and tired and spent. I had pulled an all-nighter, writing. Sweat literally dripped off me. It had smeared the ink on all the pages, but I had yet to create something that I felt confident to share with eleven talented writers with whom I was studying at a summer writers' intensive.

I never dreamed that I would be accepted into such an esteemed program in the first place. The workshop leader was an accomplished author whose work I had greatly admired. I wished I could write the way she did—deep, rich, evocative detail spun around immensely profound, literary stories. I had always aspired to become the next Edith Wharton or Willa Cather. But no matter how hard I tried, in the end my work somehow managed to veer more toward the style of Erma Bombeck and my characters the likes of Bridget Jones. I wanted to expand my horizons and break away from the comic and absurd. I wanted my work to be taken seriously.

"Send a writing sample. What have you got to lose?" my boyfriend suggested when I told him my doubts about applying to the program.

"I'm too old," I said.

"Old? Forty is the new thirty. You'll fit right in."

I smirked at him. "I'm afraid they'll laugh when they read my stuff. I hardly write serious literature."

"Why can't there be room for everyone, all types of writing?"

I just stared at him, deadpan. He didn't understand.

When I received a letter of acceptance in the mail weeks later, I feared it was the result of a clerical error. But when I showed up at the university on a hot day in June and found my name on the registration list, I knew it was for real.

On the first day of the program, my heart pounded in my throat while I listened to introductions from the eleven other writers. We were all seated at a table around the workshop leader, much like the apostles gathered around Jesus Christ at the Last Supper. I swallowed hard as my much younger peers rattled off litanies of Ivy League institutions and publishing credits from esteemed academic literary journals. I couldn't help but feel like the Thaddeus of the bunch, the least known and most forgettable of the twelve. I, too, was a college graduate—from a very small, state school. While I was a published author, my work had found its way into magazines and anthologies that I was sure none of the other writers seated around that table had ever heard of or read.

When it came time for me to introduce myself, all I managed to say was, "Hi. I think I am going to learn a lot just by breathing the same air as you people."

The room was rapt in a silence that suddenly felt never-ending. My peers, along with the workshop leader, physically leaned in my direction, as though waiting to hear the rest of my credentials. But all I could do was sit there and force a smile. I was petrified to speak another word.

Intimidated. Insecure. Out of my league. Those key words best described my feelings for four hours each day as part of the group. The writers were not only more gifted and talented than me, but also much more ambitious. When I called my boyfriend each night, I'd give him a daily update.

"More I-R-S," I'd say, using the acronym I'd devised while at the workshop to denote the plethora of stories written about incest, rape, and suicide. They were recurrent themes among the other writers in the program, and it amazed me how courageous some were to read aloud pieces that addressed those issues—some of which, I learned, were deeply personal. I didn't dare volunteer to read my stories, which seemed like insignificant little ditties in comparison.

The main thrust of the workshop delved into what makes characters unforgettable, and we dissected the traits of strong archetypes in fiction. For example, the essence of lasting and memorable characters can often be evoked simply by conjuring a name. Take Ebenezer Scrooge—a miser; Peter Pan—an eternal child unwilling to grow up; Hester Prynne—an adulteress.

During the workshop, we were all given an assignment to be completed over the course of the program. We were to take a literary archetype of our own choosing and, using a main character trait, create a story that would put the character into a situation that would specifically test that trait. On the last day of the workshop, every writer would share his or her story with the group.

With that in mind, I was inspired by one of my favorite fictional heroines, Scarlett O'Hara. I found her fascinating—colorful, headstrong, a real drama queen. She'd be perfect.

For a whole week after class, I went straight to my dorm room, intent on fashioning a serious and profound short story. I decided to focus on Scarlett being a manipulative woman in distress who insisted on getting and having her own way. But when I sat down to write, nothing jelled. I brought her back to Tara and the Civil War, but I found it immensely hard to cover new ground on the page. Even setting her in a scene of conflict with Rhett Butler, her one true love, somehow seemed tired. I even tried to plug her into the I-R-S model, but that certainly didn't feel right for Miss Scarlett.

Day after day, I wrote pages upon pages, but they were merely false starts filled with cross outs. Nothing I wrote held my interest. At 2:00 A.M. on the night before the deadline, I knew I had come up short, and I finally succumbed to the pressure and wept. There I was—a woman creeping toward middle age—sobbing in a dorm room in the wee hours of the night, sweating both literally and figuratively, over homework. Even working my hardest and trying my best, I felt beaten by inescapable mediocrity. Not knowing what else to do or where else to turn, I plucked out a few more tissues, then picked up the phone and dialed my boyfriend. I knew he was flying out on business early the next day, but I was desperate for his moral support.

"Don't you see? What you're doing is going against the grain," he told me, his gravelly voice filled with sleep. "Why don't you stop trying to be someone you're not and write the way that feels natural for you. Just have fun with it."

Fun? The word sounded completely foreign to me.

The minute I hung up the phone, I sucked back my tears. I took a deep breath, along with his advice, and began to free-write in the voice of Scarlett O'Hara herself. I took snippets of all the drama that swirled inside my own mind and decided to channel it comically through Scarlett's voice. Suddenly things started to take shape. I updated Scarlett O'Hara for the new millennium—made her over in the throes of midlife, harried and hot, and put her in the same airport my boyfriend would be departing from the next day. Scarlett's conflict would be that she'd been denied a first-class seat on the airplane—oh, tragedies of tragedies! What was a Southern Belle to do?

While the rest of the college slept, I wrote non-stop, stifling my giggles while the story poured onto the page. Then, I read and re-read the piece—tweaking it along the way—until the sky finally brightened outside my window and I hurried off to the workshop at 8:00 A.M.

Each participant's story was more seriously moving and profound than the next, and a sense of doom and dread overwhelmed me. How could the entertaining nature of my own story possibly measure up?

When I was finally called on to share my work, I stared down at my own handwriting scribbled on the page and broke out into a sick, clammy sweat. But

I cleared away the brick of fear lodged in my throat and started to read. Everyone at the table sat perfectly still as I began to tell Scarlett O'Hara's story. When my words were met with eruptions of laughter, it felt like cool breezes were suddenly rising up all around me, lifting my spirits and boosting my confidence, word by word, until I finished reading and the room burst into a shower of applause and cheering. I soared with adrenaline.

"Well, I think Kathleen's story was just the thing we all needed to cool off," the workshop leader announced after I was nominated by my peers to read the story aloud at the final reception, which would be attended by industry agents and editors. It seemed even more unbelievable than my getting into the program in the first place.

Still on a high after the workshop, I was anxious to call my boyfriend with the news. When my cell phone proved out-of-range, I found a pay phone in the dorm and immediately sat down in the booth and dialed him.

"How wonderful! I can hear you smiling," he said, thrilled to share my victory.

When I finally slipped the receiver back on the cradle, I was beaming. And I had no idea that weeks afterward, the director of the writing intensive would nominate my story for Best New American Voices (a national prize in literature) or that I would later adapt the story into a play that would be showcased off-Broadway in New York City. At that moment, I just sat in the phone booth, stunned, listening to all the coins I had inserted register down into the pay phone. Ca-ching. Ca-ching. Ca-ching. The clinking sound didn't stop. It chimed on and on until almost ten dollars in quarters poured out of the change return, into my lap. Running my fingers through all the coins, I glimpsed the reflected image of myself in the glass that encased me in the phone booth and burst out laughing. I had hit the jackpot—in more ways than one.

~Kathleen Gerard

About My Promise
to My Mother

My mother started having children at age nineteen, after she quit her new career with the Canadian Armed Forces. My parents divorced when I was nine. She loved music, always had it playing in the background. When I was a young girl her favorite song was "The Ballad of Lucy Jordan." She said it was written just for her. It's about a woman examining her life and discovering that many of the dreams she had in her youth were now never going to come to pass, having been swallowed by her choices, obligations, and responsibilities. She'd put them off too long and now it was too late. It's a sad song about regrets, and the chorus laments how, at thirty-seven, Lucy realizes she'll never drive a sports car through Paris with the wind blowing in her hair.

Whenever the song came on the radio, my mother would inevitably, at some point in the tune and with varying degrees of intensity, say to me, "You listen to this song and promise me that will never be you. Promise me you'll be braver than I was, that you'll make your dreams come true. Promise me you'll go to Paris before you're thirty-seven."

My response as the perpetually bored teenager who really didn't get it was, "Yeah, yeah, I will."

My mother passed away when I was twenty years old.

On April 9, 2005, I stopped being thirty-seven. Six days after turning thirty-eight, on April 15, I boarded an airplane for Paris. True to form, I was late, but I made it.

My former roommate flew from Seattle and met me there. Our first stop, within hours of arriving in Paris, was Notre Dame (translated: "our Lady," or "gentle Mother") Cathedral. From an ocean away it had seemed like an appropriate stop. My intent was to light a candle for my mom so she would know I was there, that I had come. I never did. Notre Dame is huge, beautiful, cold, and bustling with people. It felt as intimate as a shopping mall. If my mother had been there, I would not have heard her over the din. I traversed the interior, admired it immensely, and exited candle-less.

An ocean away, renting a sports car and driving around Paris seemed like a good idea. I didn't do that either.

Our apartment was across the river from the Eiffel Tower and a short walk away from the monument marking the entrance to the tunnel where Lady Diana crashed and died. Any questions I might have had about how Lady Diana could have had such a horrible, high-speed crash in downtown Paris were answered. Parisian drivers are nuts. We canceled the car rental.

The day before we left to return home, we blessedly visited my now-favorite spot in all of France: the Paris Opera House. We emerged from its breathtaking splendor to find a long line of cabs parked by the curb. We selected the fifth car back as the "most sporty looking" and walked up to it. The cab drivers became completely up in arms over our ignorance of the protocols of taxi queuing.

My mastery of the French language was not advanced enough to explain that the song is about driving through Paris in a sports car—not a reliable family wagon. Assuming defeat before I even began, I chose the alternate route of speaking Japanese, in which I am passable, instead, hoping at least one of the taxi drivers would just throw in the towel due to communication difficulties and let me have my way. My friend chose LOUD AMERICAN.

Between the two of us, we managed to convince the taxi mafia to drop the dogma associated with their taxi queue system and let us have the one we wanted.

When the gods want to punish you, they answer your prayers.

Our non-English-, non-French-, non-Japanese-speaking, Liberian-born taxi driver began to speed along the river toward our apartment. Soon we were zipping along with the flow of traffic and zigzagging anything that could be zigged or zagged. Normally, my hair, which reaches halfway down my back, is harmless. In the back of a sports car in Paris with the windows down, it becomes a facial laceration weapon that wraps around my tongue and flies down my throat to my larynx.

After a few minutes of wrestling with my windswept hair and overactive gag reflex, I turned to my friend and suggested we get out while the getting was good. She agreed. Apparently, the Liberian translation for "Whoa! Halt! Arret! Finito!" when yelled in stereo is, "Could you please pull over at the nearest subway station," because that's just what he did.

We spent twelve days playing tourist in Paris and the south of France. All the while, the back of my brain was waiting for a moment of "eureka," when I would know I had made the connection with my mother. The sign that she knew I had heard her plea all those years ago and had fulfilled my promise to her.

It never came. When the plane lifted off, leaving Paris behind, the disappointment was crushing. I felt like a failure.

Not one to wallow, I decided there was nothing more I could do and dropped it. I then turned my attention toward all the things that would be waiting for me when I arrived home. My two amazing children would be all over me with questions. My husband and best friend of twenty-two years would be patient until the children were in bed. Then he and I could talk about my trip and all the things we'd have to do to get ready for the next year's planting on our farm. My publisher was also waiting for me to hurry up with another set of revisions for my novel, due to be released the following spring.

A hint of light began to flicker in the back of my mind. The more I examined the light, the brighter it became. At thirty-eight, I have no regrets about my life so far. I wanted to have a happy family, and I have one. I wanted to see the world, and so far the only continents I'm missing are Antarctica and Australia. I wanted to be an author, and in April 2006, I became one. My first novel has been published, the second is complete, and I am working my way through the third.

I guess I did hear you, Mom. It just took a trip to Paris for me to realize that I had also been listening.

~Allison Maher

Memoirs of a Shiksa

Like heat-seeking missiles, they're always the first to find you, even in the thickest throng of partygoers.

"So you write screenplays?" they giddily inquire. "You know, people keep saying that my life would make a great movie."

It's at this point that I paste on my "oh, isn't that interesting" smile, hastily down the remainder of my martini, and pretend my cell phone just vibrated with an emergency page I simply must excuse myself to answer. As I tell my husband, if I had a nickel for every time someone has invited me to adapt their memoirs for the silver screen, I probably could have funded a vacation home for us in Monaco by now.

"You should just do what I do," my hairdresser recommends. Knowing that total strangers will bombard her with requests for free advice about their cut, style, or color, she artfully avoids such ambush altogether by telling them she sells shoes at Nordstrom. "A career in footwear makes for a much shorter conversation," she points out.

Writers, in contrast, are perceived as a mythic dichotomy by nonwriters. On the one hand, they're awestruck that we can make a full-time living merely by putting words to paper and stringing them into a seamless tableau. On the other hand, they assume we're walking around most of the day with empty heads that require an ongoing input of free ideas in exchange for a share of the fame. Why else, I ask myself, do I get unsolicited e-mails from students in Pakistan and housewives in Duluth who offer to tell me all the details of their life stories so I can turn them into movies and split the proceeds with them?

Yes, it's true what they say that everyone has a book inside of them. It's just as true that most of these tomes should quietly remain there. Why? Because although truth is often stranger than fiction, it's considerably less commercial and usually of riveting interest only to the person who actually lived through it.

The first (and only) time I took up the challenge of adapting a memoir was for an elderly feminist who mailed me a copy of her autobiography after following my screenwriting columns in magazines for several years. "You seem to know what you're doing," she praised, "so I've decided that you're the best qualified person for this responsibility."

Initially, I was flattered she'd sought me out. Her recollections of—and participation in—the early years of women's liberation were replete with political anecdotes and personality profiles that appealed to my love of history. And hey, let's face it, what writer doesn't want to be sought out by a fan who's enthusiastically waving a checkbook?

Conversely, the fact that her book was self-published and listed only first-name testimonials (i.e., Esther from Boca: "I couldn't put it down!") should perhaps have been a clue that Hollywood wasn't exactly beating a hasty path to her condo.

Nonetheless, her sagacity was amusing, and I saw a chance to explore the mindset of a less-liberated generation by staging a story in which a young screenwriter is hired to turn an older woman's journals into a movie.

"And, of course, I'll want your feedback along the way," I said, mistakenly assuming that her comments regarding my interpretation would make for an easier job than if my subject had been long deceased and leaving me to guesswork.

I may as well have ordered a side-smack with a two-by-four to my forehead while I was at it.

Her first criticism was that the young screenwriter

I had invented was in too many scenes. "I was thinking she could just be a voice on the phone," she said.

"But they're collaborating. That's why they're in
the same room."

"We're not in the same room," she countered.
"We're not even in the same state and it's working
out just fine. Besides," she said, "I don't want someone
upstaging me."

I diplomatically explained that the demographics
of the movie-going public would be best served if one
of the two leads were in her late twenties.

She quickly responded with a list of all the twenty-
something actresses whose talents and indiscreet life-
styles she didn't particularly care for. "What do you
think about Blythe Danner playing me?" she asked.
"Or maybe Meryl Streep. Do any of your peeps know
Meryl?"

"The casting decisions will probably be out of our
hands," I replied, sidestepping the reality that (1) I'm
not yet at a level that has peeps who blissfully do my
bidding, and (2) Dr. Ruth would be a better match if
we were going for accuracy.

"You should make a margin note and describe
my character as a 'Meryl Streep type,'" she suggested.
"That way they'll know who we want." To this ambitious wish list, she subsequently added the belief that
Lorenzo Lamas should play her first husband ("I loved

him in *Falcon Crest*"), Shania Twain should play her older daughter ("We could throw in a few songs"), and Cybil Shepherd ("Just because") should play Gloria Steinem. "And, of course, you'll want me to do some walk-ons here and there as myself and give a few speeches," she said.

Norma Desmond, it appeared, was getting ready for her close-up.

Like many fledgling authors who are fiercely possessive of their words, she also expected my 110-page script to follow her 529-page book verbatim.

"You left out the golf cart scene with Uncle Herschel," she chided.

"He was only in two paragraphs," I said.

She insisted they were pivotal to the plot. "Besides," she added, "I don't want to hurt his feelings."

I gently reminded her that he'd been dead since 1957.

"Like you don't think he'd know?" she archly replied.

I began to dread the thrice-daily arrival of e-mails with the header "Just a Few Notes." Such notes, invariably, ran longer than whatever scenes I'd sent her to review.

Creative license was a phrase foreign to her as well. "You're making up things that didn't happen," she declared.

I explained that it was to make the dated content more relevant to contemporary audiences.

"Are you saying my life's irrelevant?" she shot back. She reminded me that she'd been famous.

Even famous people, I pointed out, don't always have lives that translate well to film production. Linus Pauling, for instance, gave us quantum mechanics and molecular biology, but could he deliver two hours of Oscar-worthy entertainment? That no one's ever made a movie about him is probably with good reason.

"I've been rethinking our arrangement on the proceeds," she announced a few weeks later. "Why should it be a fifty-fifty split when you wouldn't have a story to write at all if I hadn't lived it? I'm thinking more like ninety-ten."

I'm thinking it's time to start looking for a graceful exit.

"And when we get an Academy Award," she continued, "I think it would be better if you stayed in the audience, since I have a lot of people I'm planning to thank and I don't want to run over my time limit."

She also asked me if I thought she should write to the Academy and request that Hugh Jackman be the presenter of her Oscar. The devilish side of me almost told her "yes," except that I was afraid she'd use my name and I'd never be able to work in this town again.

When last we parted, she had completely dropped the idea of the film and was planning to do a one-woman Broadway show where she'd read excerpts from her book out loud. I wished her well and made myself a mental note: Working with dead people is way easier and a lot less headache.

Oh, and the next time you see me at a party, let's talk about shoes.

~Christina Hamlett

We Are Mortified by You

You have decided to become a personal essayist. You're desperate, actually, to stop being a business journalist and to get your first essay published. So desperate, you are going to write the essay in second person.

This is not a Jay McInerney fan-gone-wild thing. It has to do with the story you want to tell, which is about the time you climbed California's Mount Shasta and your marriage nearly broke up. The problem is that you want the story to appear in the *Mountain Gazette*, the publication of choice for the climbing elite. Needless to say, you are not one of those elite, and the only way you can think of to get them to see your point of view is through brute linguistic force— dirty trick though that might be. Plus, you are grasping for something different that will make the editor notice you and publish your first essay.

You know that this first publication will require trickery, because your transition from business journalist to personal essayist has been rocky. Your husband, a former writer who once won awards, read your early efforts and told you ever so gently that he thought they were not quite ready to send to editors. You decided to remain married to him anyway. One day your neighbor's University of California Berkeley Extension catalog arrived in the mail by mistake. As you walked it over to him, you noticed a listing for a memoir class led by a Pushcart nominee. You signed up before you could change your mind. Now that the class has ended, you have succeeded in breaking many of your business journalist habits, but that doesn't mean editors are clamoring for your golden phrases just yet.

Unusual point of view in hand, you write a draft of the story. It's not about the climb itself. Who wants to read about Mount Shasta? Everest, yes. Shasta, not so much. At 14,162 feet, it's only about half an Everest, and readers of the *Mountain Gazette* would not be especially impressed. Nobody much dies on Mount Shasta. Instead, you write about the night before the climb—the horrible, unvarnished truth. It was a tough time in your marriage. You had figured out that you had a talent for hiking at altitude. This might have been a good thing, since your husband once climbed the Grand Teton—a peak much more technical than Mount Shasta. But he is five years older than you and not interested anymore. He gained a belly in law school and is too busy to work it off. But even after two kids you've still got abs, and you're feeling your thirty-something oats. You sign up for an all-women's summit attempt via the West Face Gully, and your plan is to find a bunch of buff climbers in a bar in town the night before the climb begins and flirt with them.

This is not flattering stuff, but that's the plight of the personal essayist. You write about your desire to find beer-swilling hotties who turn out not to exist.

There are two bars in town, and both are nearly empty. It's Sunday night, about 8:00; what were you thinking? You take yourself out to dinner and hunt for climbers again afterward. Nothing. You begin to realize you are behaving like an ass. You slink back to your hotel, and the next morning you begin your ascent of the snowy peak. The experience is transformative. You are an actual mountaineer, sort of.

You come home and tell your husband that your next climb will be Pico de Orizaba in Mexico, which, at 18,700 feet, is much more dangerous than Shasta. He doesn't say you can't go, but he tells you how he worried about your safety, even on a mountain as relatively benign as Shasta. He doesn't know how he will get through this, a life in which his wife will leave him and the kids once or twice a year to do something so dangerous that she might come back injured or, worse, not at all.

He makes you a deal: If you'll stay under 15,000 feet, he'll get back in shape so the two of you can climb together. And he does. Every year in July, on your anniversary, you climb another of California's 14,000-foot peaks and exchange very light gifts on the top. Marital disaster averted.

You send the story off to the editor of the *Gazette*. The usual chasing-around follows: Did he get it? Did he read it? Did he like it? Turns out he likes it so much he decides to save it for eight months so he can publish it in the August "Climbing Issue." That's the coolest issue of the year. It's a long time to wait. You're a personal essayist now—you're official—but nobody knows except you. You re-read the story more times than is healthy. Wait, should you fact-check it? You used to work at *Fortune*, where you practically got a degree in fact-checking. But this is not a business story; you're the only source, and you trust you. What's to fact-check? Well, maybe the name of the climbing store you mention: The Fifth Season. All done. You wait for August to come.

The August issue arrives in the mail, and your story is a thing of beauty. The editor has done nothing weird to it. The artist has come up with a funny illustration. You have an entire spread, two oversized pages. You are basking in glory. You want more copies to send to everyone in your extended family, but you quickly discover that the issue is sold out and there aren't any more to be had. You call The Fifth Season in hopes they will mail you some issues in gratitude for the free publicity, and you say you wrote the story that mentions their store. There's a long silence. This is not what you expected.

"Did you like it?" you ask cautiously.

"Yes, we all liked it," the clerk says. "It's just that the name of the town isn't Shasta City. It's Mount Shasta City. Shasta City is an hour away."

The title of the story is: "Looking for a Scene in Shasta City."

Your neck is hot; your heart is making a swoosh noise in your ears. Your career as a personal essayist is going to end before it can even get started. And the reason is really too ironic to enumerate: It's because, in an effort to unlearn everything you learned as a business writer at *Time Inc.*, you ignored the one lesson that applies to all writing, personal or otherwise. Fact. Check. Carefully. Just because your only source is you doesn't mean she's exempt from independent verification.

You attempt some damage control. First, you contact the editor. You tell him you're mortified. He says he's not too happy himself. He's already received several critical letters to the editor. So you write your own in an effort to make light of the situation. The story mentions your sorry sense of direction, that it has become clear to you that the reason you couldn't find the scene in Shasta City is because you weren't actually there.

It takes twenty-eight long days for the next issue to arrive and another thirty for the issue with your story's letters to come. It's worse than you thought. Not only are readers incensed that you could make such an idiotic error, they are not aware that your story was self-parody. The lines could not be juicier. A Mount Shasta City climber writes: "We are certainly not sitting in bars like zoo animals, waiting to indulge each and every yuppie who comes to town to try and slay the mountain with fake ambassadorship and regale them in trivia Q-and-A sessions."

The editor tries to make light too, coming at first to your defense. "Any time the climbers in Mt. Shasta tire of having women walking around seriously searching for male bar company, please feel free to refer them to the wonderful little mountain hamlet of Frisco, Colorado, where, if word gets out that a genuine female is out and about looking for males to hobnob with over a beer or three, entire truckloads of gentlemen will be more than happy to set aside whatever productive activities they might be engaged in and come a runnin'."

You are feeling a bit less dizzy until you read his tagline: "We are, of course, somewhat mortified about the name screw-up."

Not only will you never be allowed to write for the *Mountain Gazette* again, but the editor has used your own word against you.

It takes six months before you work up the nerve to submit another personal essay. You write a piece about how miserable you are not to be Dean Karnazes, the world-class ultramarathoner who is a dad in your daughter's fourth-grade class. You e-mail it to the My Word column of the *San Francisco Chronicle Magazine*. The editor accepts it in 25 minutes. She appears not to have heard that you don't know the difference between Shasta City and Mount Shasta City. After the story is published, the magazine prints a letter to the editor from a woman who seems not to be aware that the story was self-parody. But at least she doesn't accuse you of taking yourself too seriously in the wrong town.

~*Stephanie Losee*

A New Point of View

Words flood through my fingers onto the page. Delicious images. Sparkling ideas. Until a few minutes ago I'd been laboring uselessly on a story, ideas for it just beyond reach at the edges of my conscious mind. Every word I'd come up with had been mundane, every sentence banal. But suddenly I have become the channel for a higher creative process. Now the story is writing itself, the narrative fluid, the language rich.

"Can I ask you a question?" My husband's voice invades the room.

Instantly my muse flees. A flash of anger tightens my chest.

"Oh, sorry, Babe, you're busy writing," Ray says, putting his hands on my shoulders and peering at the computer screen. "I'll ask you later."

"You're here now," I snarl. "Go ahead."

"Wow, you're crabby today." Ray takes his hands from my shoulders. "I said I was sorry."

I am crabby, but sorry won't bring back my burst of inspiration. We've talked several times since his recent retirement about my need for uninterrupted writing time.

"Just close the door, and I won't come in," Ray says matter-of-factly. "I can't read your mind. I'll talk to you later." I watch him pad out in stocking feet, pulling the door shut behind him, and then return to my story. For a few minutes I move my fingers on the keyboard, but the new ideas are vague, the words lifeless. Discouraged, I push my chair back from the desk.

I'm crabby, Ray's crabby—not what I want. Just close the door, Ray had said. Is the answer to the problem of uninterrupted time really so simple? Often, when I'm paying bills or answering e-mails, I don't mind his questions. Can a daughter from out of town stay the weekend? Is Friday clear for a golf game? Nothing's on the calendar, but he wants to make sure. This morning I minded his intrusion very much, but he had no way of knowing not to disturb me.

Over the next few weeks I practice closing the door when I'm planning to seriously write. It proves a surprisingly difficult task. When I close the door, shutting Ray out, I feel selfish and rude. Both my tabby and my golden retriever like to sneak in and out, which theoretically might disturb me, but brightens me instead, and closing the door shuts them out too. Sometimes I have a book in one hand and a cup of tea in the other when I enter my office, or I'm so lost in an idea that I simply forget the door.

But more and more often, when I'm juggling all the parts of an essay in my head or trying to enliven a bit of stodgy prose, I remember to close it.

One afternoon, the door closed per our agreement, I settle in to finish a short-story revision. I'm up against a deadline and am thanking all the gods of the creative process that the words are singing on the page. The door clicks open. "Do you want to go with us for a walk on the waterfront?" Ray asks, walking in, a green dog leash dangling from his hand.

The song ends mid-measure. I hold back various sharp retorts with tight lips, take a deep breath, and say, "Did you notice the door?"

"Yeah, I did, but it's such a beautiful day. Blue sky, perfect temperature. I'm taking the dog and thought you'd want to come too."

Ordinarily I would want to go, but I have this deadline. Right now nothing tempts me but trying to entice back the muse.

"By the way, you don't know how many times I do walk away when I see your signal," Ray says. "But this seemed worth interrupting."

It might to anyone but a writer. "If you wait an hour, I'll join you," I say.

"I want to catch the good sun. We'll see you for dinner." Ray shuts the door behind him.

I slog through the rest of the story, but I can't get back quite the same upbeat tone. I'm frustrated and disappointed with the end result.

That evening I call two artist friends who have talked about similar difficulties in finding uninter-rupted time for their work. One is a watercolorist who claims she has told her telecommuting husband a mil-lion times that she is not his executive assistant, she is an artist. I learn that she has recently calendared every weekday morning from eight to twelve for her painting, and her husband has promised to honor that.

I realize that many writers discipline themselves to work on a regular morning schedule, but Ray and I bike on Wednesday mornings with a group of friends, and Thursday mornings we have yoga. Besides, the muse doesn't tap my shoulder at the same time every day. I can sit down at a preplanned time and take care of some writing tasks, but I want a way to also protect the bursts of creative juices that, when uninterrupted, often produce my best work.

I call my other friend, who is a ceramicist. He has often bemoaned how difficult it is to find time in his home studio because of his wife and children's efforts to involve him in their activities. He tells me he has purchased one of those clocks seen on doors of shops that say "I'll be back" and show the time in big red hands. That way both his wife and children will know at what time he will be available. It's working for them, but I'm pretty sure Ray would be offended if I hung a clock with big red hands outside my office door. We need to find our own solution.

Yet again I broach the subject of the closed door with Ray. I expect him to get defensive, since he's heard it all before. But he doesn't sound defensive, just reasonable, when he listens to my spiel and then says quietly, "You know, I have needs too."

I pause. Of course he has needs too. Have I only been thinking of myself? "I figure the closed door is as good a thing for you as it is for me," I stammer. "It means you are totally free to do whatever you want without my interference."

"But you're determining when that free time will be, not me. When you take on a writing project, I don't have any say in the times we can be together."

Wow. For the first time I see the issue from his side. I've had no idea how dictatorial I am. We're supposed to be partners. I admit that I've been known to leave dinner half prepared and run to my computer when a fabulous idea strikes, but I try to get back to my cooking as soon as I've got the idea down. Part of me wants to apologize to Ray for all former hurts and promise him we'll calendar all my writing time together. Another part of me feels like, Hey, I do that, and I toss my writing career down the laundry chute.

"I'm not asking you to follow some rigid schedule," Ray says. "I know you don't work like that. But maybe if you know something is coming up you could warn me."

I exhale and look at Ray with profound appreciation. I think I see wings sprouting from his shoulders while a golden halo shapes itself around his head. He's trying to respect me as hard as I'm trying to respect him.

"All you're asking is that I check with you before I write?"

"When you know a few days out that a big project is coming up, you could tell me so I can plan to play golf or something. And I would like some time with you every day that I can count on, even if it's just lunch or a glass of wine before dinner. I thought retirement would mean more time together. I miss you when you're in your writing world."

The glass of wine before dinner appeals to me more than lunch together, because the muse is apt to beckon midday no matter when I sit at my desk. But if it doesn't, I could surprise Ray with a sandwich to share. I have some changing to do. All couples have those areas where they need to negotiate, and I seem to have hit one of ours. Writing is a solitary activity, but I don't live alone. Next time I tackle a writing project that requires my complete attention, if at all possible I will talk to Ray first about my need to go to my office and invite in my muse. I think we can find a time that works for both of us and for that glass of wine and walk on the waterfront too.

~Samantha Ducloux Waltz

Of Rewrites and Restitution

As a beginning writer I tried to do everything right. I used positive visualization techniques to picture my upcoming success. I imagined myself on the phone talking to my hot-shot New York agent, and then I pictured putting him on hold because Oprah was on the other line. To vary the fantasy, I'd sometimes picture myself acting demure as I accepted the National Book Award or the Pulitzer Prize. I even knew who I would thank and in what order. My speeches were tasteful and modest.

When I wasn't busy visualizing, I tried my hand at writing. Then I wrote some more. I practiced writing similes using food smells. I joined a writers' group and went to classes and seminars, inhaling information like it was the aroma of fresh-baked bread.

I wrote and rewrote and wrote again, and submitted my work as if postage was a pittance. Each piece was sent out lovingly with the hope that some savvy editor would be smart enough to recognize just what he held in his hands. When I eventually made it big, the first one who published me would be able to say they'd launched my career.

That would be one lucky, lucky editor.

Then I got it—the call. A national publication wanted to publish a piece I wrote about my family's recent triumph over a problem in our community. I played it cool, thanked the editor for calling, hung up and thought of the multitudes who would read my words. Who knew how many people would be moved by my story? It was really an auspicious start for a beginner, not that I didn't deserve it.

About a week later, another editor from the magazine called (from New York!) to talk about my story. I'll call him Bob.

Lucky, lucky Bob.

Bob was doing a bit of rewriting on the story, just a bit, and thought it would be good to give the reader a little background information, so that when they got to the part of the story with the big problem they would really feel for this wonderful family.

Bob was my new best friend, and if Bob said we needed background information, who was I to quibble? I talked as if on sodium pentothal and told Bob everything he wanted to know. It wasn't until he asked how my husband and I had met that I started to wonder how far back he wanted to go.

"You're a little nosy, aren't you, Bob?" I asked jokingly. By this time we were like old friends.

"Well," he said, "sometimes I think my job encompasses more than just editing. I like to get into the psychology behind people's actions and see what really makes them tick."

How lucky for me, I thought. *My first exposure to an editor of a national publication, and he really cares about people.* I made a mental note to add Bob to my Christmas card list.

I had five short months to wait until the magazine came out, but in the meantime I was just a little too excited to keep the news to myself, so I told a few writing buddies. Then, since my husband and kids knew, I really had to tell the relatives. One of the kids was sure to spill the beans, and it would sound so much better coming from me. After that, the circle widened a little more when I told a few nonwriter friends. This was my chance to show them that all the time and money spent on classes, writing supplies, postage, and so on, had really paid off.

"Six hundred dollars!" I told them.

"Wow!" they said.

I'd still be up on a cloud today if I hadn't retrieved the e-mail attachment Bob sent me a few weeks later.

The story he sent had a similar scenario to mine, and the people had the same names as the members of my family. I was confused until I read his memo: "Karen, here are the finished rewrites. I think it's a very touching piece."

A touching piece? I was livid. His version contained conversations and events that had never happened. He'd fictionalized my life. I counted: only four sentences of mine survived the carnage.

This couldn't be what writing was all about, I thought. I had integrity. There was no way I would allow this. He could just forget the whole thing.

"Whoa, Nellie," my husband said. Or something like that. "Think of the money. Think of the writing credit." And last, "Christmas is coming."

"But look at this," I said, pointing to Bob's handiwork. "This isn't how we talk. He made us sound like idiots."

I wailed and moaned and made everyone I knew read both versions and tell me mine was better. The ones who didn't agree were banished from my life forever. I'm really going to miss Dad.

In the end, I did what any self-respecting beginner would do: I sold out. My compromise was that I made a few changes to Bob's story. We did an editor/writer reversal.

During my last phone conversation with Bob, I mentioned my disappointment with how the story was handled.

"Writing is a collaborative process," he told me. "Even if I were to write a story for this magazine, other editors would change things. Our readers have certain expectations, and we know best how to make sure they're met."

That's what he said, but what I heard was, "You're a loser, and your writing sucks." Clearly he had not heard he was dealing with a future National Book Award winner.

We exchanged pleasantries before we said our final goodbye.

"It was nice working with you, Karen."

"It was nice working with you too, Bob." That's what I said, but what I meant was, *Eat dirt, Bob.* In the nicest possible way, of course.

Not long after that I had an article accepted by the local paper. The editor, Sue, was most complimentary and asked me to write for them on a regular basis. Sue really liked my work.

Lucky, lucky Sue.

~*Karen McQuestion*

Me, an Artist

I claimed my title today. It was like a fairy tale: the kind in which the young prince or princess, brought up with no external acknowledgment, goes through travails that reveal his or her true nature. To keep things interesting, the details of the character-testing struggle vary, but these tales usually wrap up with the hero claiming a throne and throwing a blow-out party complete with flaming torches and lots of brocade.

My experience was a momentous occasion just like that, although without festivities or the pealing of bells across the kingdom. I was brushing my teeth, looking into my eyes in the mirror, and feeling a wonderful lightness of spirit. I said to myself for the first time, "I am an artist." Then I rinsed.

I'd known it long before. As a little girl I was dazzled by a day when the cold had encased every single twig in a tiny shell of ice. Every thing—from the berries that clung to the barberry bushes to the pale yellow railings of our porch—had its own delicate icing, frozen in minute and boundless perfection. I tried to capture the beauty of that day in words. Somehow I knew that my desire to share my vision of how things looked and felt meant I was an artist.

But "artist" seemed too boastful a word. I didn't dare use it, censoring myself before others could, anxious not to be criticized for my presumption. I feared people would see it as their duty to "take me down a peg," in the phrase they used then for character assassination. I knew that struggling to sketch my experience with words made me feel alive to the world in a way unlike any other, but I suspected it wasn't something most kids did.

My little peers somehow knew the truth about me: "You talk like a book," they teased. They meant to insult me by saying I was different, and therefore, in the logic of kids, wrong. Behind the sneering tone, I heard an acknowledgment of the word I longed to claim, even though it set me apart from them. The adults in my world didn't use my beautiful word either; they said I was "different." Now I can see how they projected their own insecurities onto me, conditioning me to limit my horizons, reduce my expectations, and abandon dreams that didn't have a clear path to payoff. I heard many times that artists and writers were hapless, starving creatures, and that message still shapes my immediate reactions. The other day I saw a van with a license plate that said, 2WRITRS and my first thought was, "Yeah, but only one car!"

I bought the line that I couldn't support myself as a creative writer. Unfortunately, I simply couldn't imagine any other job. My mother threw up her hands and said, "There's money in computers." So I became a marketing writer specializing in high tech. I was writing, yes, but I wasn't creating. I didn't dare aim any higher.

I prospered, but every few years I would be overwhelmed by a feeling that I was wasting my time. When those moments came, I never considered joining the Peace Corps, changing jobs, or leaving my partner. I knew what I needed. I would start to write fiction, essays, and poems. After just a few days of writing for an hour or so, ideas would start coming at me from all directions. Vacuuming, I bumped a book out of its place on the shelf, and that served as the start for an essay on my father. A curtain blowing in the breeze took on a shape that became the central image for a short story. I scribbled notes on scraps of paper, typed stories, and felt a deep sense of replenishment.

Then something would happen to disrupt my writing routine, and I would stop. I could blame events and crises in a busy life, but that would be dishonest. Through all those same events and crises I showed up at the gym two or three times a week, with only minimal pauses to heal injuries or give birth. I stuck with my workout routine because I thought it was worthwhile, but I didn't stand by my desire to write my own material because I wasn't convinced of its value.

What can my writing possibly add to the world and its struggles? I would ask myself sternly. *Look at a bookstore: so many books, so many voices. Surely there are enough. Who needs another?* Writing personal musings or stories as insubstantial as air seemed a frivolous use of my precious time on earth.

I would stop. Years would pass. Slowly the yearning would build again, until I allowed myself a few hours at the keyboard, working for no client, singing to myself. And now I am beginning again, following an inner voice that sometimes shapes into a song and sometimes just grumbles about the day. I'm noticing how good it feels. Not easy, but good. Satisfying. These few hours are the yeast that rises up and lightens the greater mass of hours I devote to my work, family, and even the gym.

My writer's mind has been exploring the feeling. And so the other night, while brushing my teeth, the observation crossed my mind: I am someone who does not feel complete unless I regularly spend time on creative writing. People who do not feel complete unless they spend time on creative expression are called "artists." Artists are driven to look at things their own way and share that vision, and are unhappy when they don't follow that impulse. Artists are deeply nourished by things others overlook: a shape, a splash of color, a few words.

"I am an artist," I said through the toothpaste as the realization hit me. I waited for a moment. The glass slipper slid on the foot, the sword came free of the stone, the locked doors rumbled open at the voice of the heir. I'd dared to claim my title. I was no longer "different"—an uneasy word—I was an artist, and suddenly I belonged to a group after all.

~Meridian James

Falling in Love Again

I've fallen in love with a writer. Again. Only this time, it may be serious.

I've been falling in love with writers since I learned to read at the age of five. Sitting on my mother's lap, I followed her finger with my eyes as she intoned the silly syllables of Dr. Seuss, my first love. I fell hard—what girl hasn't?—for his wit, his whimsy, his wanton way with the written word. Some forty years later, I can still recite his magnum opus, *One Fish Two Fish Red Fish Blue Fish*, in its entirety, from memory. And still cry at the beauty of it.

By the time I was seven, the raucous rhymes of Dr. Seuss were no longer enough to keep my exclusive interest. There were more fish in the sea, more than I could count, right in that wonderful ocean of books called the local library. There I discovered writers who wrote books about boys and girls just like me doing fantastic things: Frank Baum and Dorothy, Donald J. Sobel and Encyclopedia Brown, E. B. White and Fern. I flirted wildly with all of these writers, but grew serious about none. For there was no one writer to whom I would pledge my deepest, darkest young passion. Capturing my Jungian little heart required double the literary delectability—and I found it in the Brothers Grimm. Night after night, I shined a flashlight under my covers to illuminate the gruesome, magical tales of love and loss, journey and justice, hamartia and heroism.

This love affair with the Grimm boys went on for years. But finally I grew tired of the patriarchic promises inherent in once upon a time and happily ever after. There was more to life beyond the castle walls, even for us princesses. I found myself drawn to writers who could show me what that life could be— smart, funny, compassionate women who seduced me with their daring heroines: Carolyn Keene and Nancy Drew, Louisa May Alcott and Jo, Jane Austen and Elizabeth. No more moats for me; I'd break all the rules and still meet my Mr. Right. Right? Maybe.

By college, the mere concept of Mr. Right seemed obsolete. As I grew into womanhood, I fell in love with women writers who celebrated being female. Time for literary experimentation! I was flying with Erica Jong, christening the women's room with

Marilyn French, exploring my secret garden with Nancy Friday. Move over, male writers: make room for the sacred feminine!

Sooner or later, the sacred feminine leads to the Big M: Motherhood. Becoming a mom brought me back to literary equilibrium. I reread all my old favorites to my children, bumping into all those old loves with affection and admiration. And while my babies slept, I immersed myself in a sensual bath of muscular prose by the Johns: Cheever, Updike, Irving. I lost myself in Shakespeare, Hemingway, Fitzgerald, and all the women who wrote as men, notably George Sand and George Eliot.

Like many avid readers, I longed to learn to write myself. While my babies napped, I wrote essays, reviews, articles, short stories, even a novel. I took classes at night and joined a writers' group. Most important, I started to read as a writer, and the reading fed my writing even as the writing fueled my reading.

When my children reached school age, I went to work in publishing—first as a writer and later as an editor, beginning a career-long dalliance with more writers than I can count or even remember. As an editor and writer, my world is words and my heroes are wordsmiths. Every day brings new writers to fall for—and I fall for them on a regular basis. After more than twenty years in the business, I'm still a sucker for a good writer.

But for all the writers I've known and loved, I've never dated one. I suppose it's not surprising that eventually I'd lose my heart to a living, breathing writer who could grace my life as well as the page. I met him at a writers' conference, where we were both speakers. He was as silly as Dr. Seuss, as profoundly male as Hemingway, as entertaining as the Brothers Grimm. A literate cowboy from Wyoming, he was as grounded in his wild places as the Johns were in theirs. It was love at first word—like reading Pablo Neruda for the first time.

I love to read his work—and he loves to read mine. As an editor who has spent her days polishing other writers' work, the writer in me had been relegated to nights for years. Over time I'd begun to think of myself as an editor first and a writer second. But falling in love with a writer has reminded me that I was a writer first—and always will be. His passion and commitment to storytelling has inspired me to tell my own stories again.

So, pens in hand, we've begun our once-upon-a-time. Whether we turn out to live happily ever after or not doesn't really matter. What matters, in the end, is the story itself. Because the story is the gift all writers leave behind, a labor of love to be savored, word by word, until The End.

~Paula Munier

The Writer Who Couldn't Read

I was on a temporary two-week job with the post office during the Christmas crunch when I entered Mr. Stanley's bookshop for the first time. Rows of homemade pine shelves crammed with books towered over more books spilling out of cardboard cartons stacked on the linoleum floor. The "checkout" was an old oak desk with a manual black Underwood typewriter mounted on a built-in tray and a marble-topped cash register that had "No Sale" in its window.

When I walked in, I was greeted with the smell of dust mixed with the mellow, dry-corn fragrance of old books. Then came the aroma of freshly brewed tea as I watched the old bookseller come into the shop from his connecting three-room flat. Balancing two large mugs of hot tea in one hand, this survivor of Depression-era polio maneuvered through the maze of cartons with a sailor's rocking gait, shifting his weight between his cane and a scarred leather block of a shoe that evened out his right leg. Sharing a cup of tea with his regular mail carrier was a ritual with Mr. Stanley, but this day he would share it with me, changing my life forever.

Almost a decade earlier, while still a boy of thirteen, I had taken what I could carry in a small brown suitcase and headed for the nearest highway, escaping a world where a father's lessons were taught with fists. During the years that followed, I'd hitched around the country, lived for brief periods with a number of kind people, done a tour in the Marines, and worked the odd jobs of a young man who'd never graduated from school. While I was burning daylight, my peers back home graduated high school, perhaps college, and started families. Awaiting me after the holidays was another job in another warehouse.

In Mr. Stanley's mail was a magazine for writers. I had no idea that such a magazine existed, and I asked him if he were a writer. He said that perhaps in time he would be and that his true love was poetry. I told him I'd had thoughts of being a writer myself someday, and Mr. Stanley, his face lighting up, eagerly invited me to come and see him when I had time.

For several days I drank my tea and ate my lunch

in the Amphora Bookshop, listening to Mr. Stanley's stories and sometimes a poem or two, telling him some of my adventures while on the road. At the time, I could read enough to get by, but my reading level was far below that of an adult. This came up during one of our sessions, when Mr. Stanley said, "You know, Chris, you remind me of my good friend Jack London." (I would soon learn that Mr. Stanley always spoke of writers as his good friends.)

I'd never heard the name before, and I told Mr. Stanley I'd be glad to meet his friend when he came into the shop. Mr. Stanley laughed, took a book from the barrister bookcase directly behind him, and handed it to me. "This is Jack London," he told me. Then he asked me to open the book to the first page and read out loud London's description of a sailor caught out of his element in the house of a wealthy and educated family.

As I stumbled over the words, Mr. Stanley cleared his throat and finally stopped me. "You don't read very well, do you?" he said and reached across the desk to lift the book out of my hands. "And you want to be a writer?"

I felt my face flush; I didn't answer.

"You really don't know who Jack London is?" he asked.

I shook my head.

"Rudyard Kipling?" Again I shook my head. "I guess I never had much time to read books."

The old bookseller was quiet for a few moments, and then he took a huge, shuddering sigh of air. "Well, then," he said, "we'll have to do something about that, won't we?"

Mr. Stanley offered to teach me to read properly and to educate me. Then, he told me, if I had something to say, I might become a writer. In return I would help him get his shop in order and run it a couple evenings a week and some Saturdays. It was an offer I could not refuse, and we started that night. Because I was drawn to the sea, Mr. Stanley began my lessons with illustrated books about the ocean and ships. Then we moved on to the first "real" book we would read together: Rachel Carson's *The Sea Around Us*.

Over the next three years, I met many of Mr. Stanley's friends: London (the book Mr. Stanley had handed me that day was *Martin Eden*), Steinbeck, Blanding, Service, Conrad, Kipling, Maugham, MacInnis, Plath, Oates, Kumin, Fleming, Cheever, Mailer, Welty, Vonnegut (many moons later I would receive a nice letter from the latter, welcoming me to the family of writers, after the release of my book, *Mississippi Odyssey*, which was not yet an inkling during my days in Mr. Stanley's bookshop). And through the pages of a set of books known as The Harvard Classics, Mr. Stanley introduced me to Plato, Socrates, Dante, Whitman, Browning. Then he threw in Sir Herbert Read's *To Hell with Culture*.

It was the days of wine and whitefish and cheddar and of midnight hours filled with lectures and debates, which planted the seeds for the articles and stories I would later write. It was the greatest adventure of my life.

With the help of Mr. Stanley's books, I also taught myself photography and still work as a freelance photographer to buy my writing time. Mr. Stanley lived to see me publish, and to critique my work and to teach some more. Then, when I thought I was ready, I began work on a novel, autobiographical, of course. While working up my notes and outlining experiences long buried, memories rose up like banshees, not angels. Fear and anger and resentment threatened to derail me, and I told Mr. Stanley I'd have to get on the road awhile to shake off the demons.

I went to the Mississippi River with my camera, hitchhiked boat rides on the river, and then spent time hitching along its banks. In time, my first book, *Mississippi Odyssey*, was born. I could not wait to get "home" and tell Mr. Stanley. But when I got there, the shop was empty, had been for months. Mr. Stanley had passed away in his sleep surrounded by his "friends." Another friend and bookseller had settled Mr. Stanley's matters and scattered his ashes in the sea. He gave me the Harvard Classics that Mr. Stanley had used to save me, the "Stanley High University" sign I had tacked over the armchair where I'd spent so many hours making so many authors my friends, and a scrapbook I'd never seen. The scrapbook contained copies of the few articles I had published thus far as well as my first short story, "The Picture Maker," which was published years later in *Modern Short Stories*. Written on the cover in Mr. Stanley's broad script were the words, "My friend, Chris Markham."

~*Chris J. Markham*

Potty Talk

My relatives drop stories round the table like bumper-crop zucchini in July. Getting a word in edgewise is harder than scoring Grandma Rosie's last biscotti. I, a quiet watcher, have always felt content to be surrounded by a crowd of entertainers, listening to their personal, true-life tales of magical trees, daring voyages, miraculous coincidences, lion-hearted forebears, and much, much more. As a child, I imagined that some born babbler and I had been accidentally switched in the hospital, though I didn't mention my theory to anyone for fear the error might be corrected. Some poor kid was probably going nuts in my birth family of stiffs, while I—lucky devil—merrily played with passels of freewheeling cousins and stopped now and then to listen to the adults telling tales of mishap and adventure.

Recently, I decided that growing up a wallflower in a family of yakkers had another advantage besides entertainment: It made me an observer of life lessons that I later carried to my writing, especially to my favorite kind of writing (about relationships). Correctly or incorrectly, I credit my family for this—blame or honor, they're free to decline.

Special honor goes to my favorite, Aunt Pauline (passed from this world and conveniently silent, unable to defend herself), because she smoked. By patriarchal decree, our clan considered smoking taboo. My grandfather had deemed it an unhealthy addiction and led by example when he unceremoniously kicked the habit himself. Devoted husband and father to my grandmother and their four daughters, he dedicated himself to worrying constantly about their health and well-being, even into the girls' adulthood. It went without saying—rare among my kin—that smoking was beyond the pale.

In deference to her father, Pauline pretended she didn't smoke. For love of his daughter, Grandpa pretended to believe her. The whole family—including us kids—knew the score and didn't discuss it. In this fictive way, Grandpa and Pauline spared each other (and the rest of us) unproductive sparring. Family harmony was preserved.

Holidays and other occasions when the family gathered at Grandma and Grandpa's, my Aunt Pauline would periodically withdraw to the bathroom—

trailed by her younger, nonsmoker sisters—to sneak a cigarette or two and gab. If, during these retreats, my cousins or I needed a mother and didn't see her right off, we knew just where to find her: the bathroom. We didn't know what exactly our mothers did there, but when one of us knocked, peals of laughter halted and perfume mixed with wisps of smoke wafted from the cracked door. For years, we kids could only wonder at the secrets behind the bathroom door.

Finally, the day arrived when we older girl-cousins knew we'd grown from "little" to "big." Teenage women-in-training, we were admitted for short intervals inside the inner sanctum. There, we discovered a womanly world reassuringly familiar yet intriguingly different.

My aunts and mother, away from the men, had a different way of talking, different stories to tell. Stripping pantyhose, picking a hangnail, using the toilet, peering in the mirror to remove bits of spinach wedged between their teeth, they described embarrassments, boasted victories, admitted mistakes, rehashed failures—stories they rarely divulged to anyone outside their circle. I felt happy and honored to be allowed to openly eavesdrop.

Pauline's smoking and the sisters' potty talks taught me basic principles—nothing affected or earth-shattering, but all down-to-earth and real—that have helped me in life and at writing. Here's what I learned:

1. **No one is perfect.** Smoking seemed to me a nasty, far-from-appealing habit, but I have a few nasty, far-from-appealing habits myself. Aunt Pauline—the eldest sister, with a heart of gold, magnificent humor, beautiful expressive features, and flair for storytelling—possessed wonderful tolerance for my own less-than-sterling qualities, and I loved her. Foibles are a part of human nature and make us—and the characters in our stories—more embraceably human.

2. **Relationships are three-dimensional.** Grandpa had an iron will; Pauline was a rebel. Both were good, strong-spirited, loving people—often at miserable loggerheads. They endured decades of tension over her smoking and sundry other disagreements, but that didn't stop them from loving each other. Relationships are shaped by past, present, and potential interactions, positive and negative; hurts and healing; affection and friction. Mixed with the blood and sweat of pain and anger—surviving beyond even faith and hope—love can endure.

3. **Everyone has secrets.** One of my cousins grew up to conclude, "Secrets are sick." I believe we all hold at least a few secrets, stories we sometimes entrust (wisely or not) to

others. What we choose to reveal about ourselves, when and how we choose to reveal it, is largely determined by our audience and the level of trust we feel. I'm grateful we heard our mothers' revealing stories, told in their down-and-dirty, authentic, sister-to-sister talk.

4. **Stories sustain us.** Life is hard. Problems are tough. Fate disappoints. But loving connections lift us, dust off our demons, and give us what we need to go on. After my mother suffered from cancer and died, Aunt Pauline continued her decline from diabetes and kidney failure, and I feared I would never know joy again. But Pauline, blind and bedridden, needed comfort and inspiration.

I harvested anecdotes from my daily life (often examples of my twittiness or stubborn perseverance), jotting them on a notepad by the phone or on pieces of paper stuffed into my purse. Then, as Pauline and I chatted, I would conversationally "recall" my ministories. She recounted her victories and frustrations, and I recounted mine. I rejoiced and sympathized, and she did too. We occasionally cried, but mostly we giggled, chuckled, chortled, howled, and roared in the face of life's challenges. Somewhere, in the sharing of our stories, in our laughter and even irreverence, we sensed something divine.

People sharing their experiences hold humanity together.

Pauline quit smoking long before she died. Grandpa was still alive to see it. I'm glad they each passed from this life knowing she'd conquered cigarettes.

After her death, I began writing stories, stories about love, loss, and holding onto dreams, but mostly about the magical, daring, miraculous, lionhearted nature of love.

Now, I imagine Pauline, free of her potty confines, regaling angels with her stories and stopping now and then to read over my shoulder as I tap, tap, tap out a stream of my own tales. Still the quiet watcher among my storytelling clan, I get my two cents in by writing. Sweet morning air wafts through my window to where I sit at my laptop—and somewhere in my tappity-tapping, I hear a tiny peal of laughter, Aunt Pauline rejoicing.

~*Marla Doherty*

Something to Say

S ometimes I think that getting published was the worst thing that ever happened to my writing.

Publication. It's what every writer wants. The Holy Grail of freelancers. To see our name in print. To agonize over just the right words for our bio. To buy five copies for our mothers. To be able, when asked, "What do you do?" followed by the inevitable, "Have you been published?" to say resoundingly, "Yes! Yes, I have."

But when it finally happened to me, things changed somehow. After years of writing for my own enjoyment, after lining the walls of my laundry room/office ceiling-to-floor with rejection letters, I finally got the call I wanted. Then another. And another. Sold three essays in three months—bada bing! Then I started getting assignments for articles as well. Editors gave me their direct lines and personal e-mail addresses.

I'd go to the mailbox, and where once only rejection letters had been, there were now contracts and magazines with my writing inside. (Okay, there were still rejection letters too. Some things never change.)

The problem was, now that I was not only writing but selling what I wrote, now that actual living, breathing people were reading my stuff, it was hard to stay focused on why I'd started writing in the first place. Back in the day, I wrote because I had something to say. There were messages, ideas, opinions inside of me that just had to get out. My kids were young and motherhood was so raw—in a million wonderful ways—that I had to write or bust.

Becoming a mom at thirty was the most exhilarating, exhausting, life-giving, draining, confirming, confusing thing I'd ever done. I loved it, but it was hard. Add to that my decision to stay home full-time, the closeness of my first two babies, the location of our house (about twenty miles from civilization), and my husband's workaholic tendencies—and the first three years of motherhood were grueling for me. I made it through with my sanity intact, largely due to the friends I found and clung to for dear life. And also because of my writing.

When I finally came up for air, around the time my third child was born, I was haunted by the idea that there was someone else out there going through what

I'd just survived. I had an image of a new mom just as madly in love with her kids as I was, but also just as insecure, just as overwhelmed, and just as desperately lonely as I'd been. I couldn't shake the thought that I could help her. If only I could tell her everything I'd learned and let her know that someone understands, maybe she'd have an easier time of it than I'd had.

So I wrote. I wrote to her. I wrote, and I wrote, and I wrote. There were so many things she needed to know. I had to tell her that losing your temper doesn't make you a bad mom. That it's okay not to know what you're doing half the time. I wanted to tell her that I knew how much she loved her kids, loved being home with them, even if she cried herself to sleep some nights. I wanted to share with her all the secrets I'd learned, to encourage her to find some friends like mine. But mostly I wanted her to know that someone understood what she was going through. And I wasn't giving up until I got the word out there where she could find it. She's what kept me plugging away in the face of so much rejection. As long as she was out there, I wouldn't stop trying to reach her.

Then it happened. I started selling essays and getting article assignments. I received phone calls from total strangers—other moms who'd read what I'd written and called to thank me for writing it. Each time, I wanted to say, "It's you! You got my message!" I started getting checks too, and that was pretty cool. I could buy my kids the extras we'd been doing without. For the first time, we could go to the movies and the Children's Museum. I could buy them new clothes rather than only secondhand stuff from the thrift store.

The more I sold, the more I wanted to sell. I bought books to tell me how to do what I was already doing, books that told me what editors want, what they look for, and what they buy. The more extra money I brought into the family coffers, the more I forgot how we'd gotten along without it. The more essays and articles I sold, the more it burned me up when my ideas were rejected. I'd flip through magazines and smirk at articles by other writers, "Humph, I could've written that." Sometimes a magazine would turn down my idea, and then four months later I'd see the same topic among their pages and feel incensed.

I wrote about topics that didn't interest me in the least. Overblown preschool graduations? I'd never been to one, but I found people who had and cranked out an article. Thumb sucking? I hadn't raised a thumb-sucker, but how hard could that be? Churned that one out too.

Rejection letters started to exasperate me. After all, didn't they know who I was? Hadn't they seen my writing clips?

I joined a writers' group and was the only published author in the bunch. I felt superior until I started listening to the things the other women wrote. A couple had real talent. Others were pedestrian, at best. But all of them wrote with passion. Their writing was angry, chilling, sexy, sweet, or provocative. I became reluctant to read my own stuff at our meetings and secretly decided the other women looked down on me. Although they all claimed to want to be published, they didn't do much about it. I'd advise them about submissions, and they'd make a half-hearted attempt now and again, but mostly they just wrote. It seemed to be enough for them. It wasn't enough for me.

One week, the day of our meeting rolled around, and I had nothing to present. I'd been working on yet another article about potty training that had taken up all my time. I started searching around my computer for something old I might read to the group. I found essays I'd written back in that laundry room when my kids were younger. (I had a full-fledged office by then.) I was astounded at how good the writing was.

I'd figured I'd learned a lot over the past few years. Turns out I'd been forgetting. I'd forgotten how to write from my gut, how to open a vein and let what's inside spill out. I'd forgotten I had something to say. Where was my message? Where was my opinion? Where was my passion? I'd abandoned that other mom long ago, the one I'd wanted to help. I'd started thinking only how to give editors what they wanted, what they'd pay for. Nowadays, as I perched my fingers over the keyboard with a new idea, I'd ask myself who was going to buy it. If the answer was "nobody," I'd write something else, regardless of whether I had an opinion on the topic.

Where's that other mom now? Who's telling her the things she needs to know? Is she feeling as alone as I did then, twelve years ago? Clearly, I'd let her down. I looked at the list of articles I was working on. Discipline. Teething. Separation anxiety. I called one of my favorite editors and told her I had an essay I wanted her to consider. The topic was mom friends, why we need each other. As soon as it's written, I'd send it to her. I've already decided, if she doesn't buy it, I'll keep submitting it until someone does. If I can't sell it for $1,000, I'll sell it for $20. If I can't sell it for $20, I'll give it away. When I'm finished with that one, I'm writing another one from the heart. I still have something to say, and there's still a mom out there who needs and wants to hear it. Yes, I still write for publication and money. But above all, I'm writing for her.

~Mimi Greenwood Knight

The Drowning Girl

B ookstores are my church," I told a friend on our way to hear author Beth Kephart read at a local bookstore. "I know it's corny, but readings are like sermons. They inspire me, get me through those days when I just want to give up writing."

Before then I'd read only Kephart's first book, *A Slant of Sun*, a memoir about her son's early years and the discovery that he had a pervasive developmental disorder, a condition on the autism spectrum. I had loved the book—both for its tender story of a mother introducing her son to the world and for the author's poetic language.

That night Kephart was promoting her fifth book, *Ghosts in the Garden: Reflections on Endings, Beginnings, and the Unearthing of Self*, a book very different from her others. While her first three books are memoirs and her fourth book is about nurturing imagination in children, *Ghosts in the Garden* is a collection of reflective essays. These lyrical essays were inspired by her visits to a public garden and her contemplation of life's lessons while there. The book is about sitting still and learning to see again.

That is all I knew of Beth Kephart when Suzanne and I went to the reading. I didn't care what her new book was about; I just wanted to meet the woman who had written such a beautiful story about her relationship with her son. A story I was eager to read again, because I had just learned that my son, too, had a condition that placed him on the autism spectrum, Asperger's syndrome.

When we arrived at the store, Suzanne and I each bought Kephart's new book and then set off to browse the new release shelf. We saw Kephart arrive, and like teenage groupies, nudged each other. In her mid-forties, Kephart had thick, almost wild, shoulder-length auburn hair, and she was wearing a crinkly chartreuse jacket over white slacks. The color of her shoes—canvas flats—matched perfectly the hue of her jacket. But it was her eyes that struck me the most, so deeply set they were thrown into shadow.

Suzanne and I followed the entourage through the bookstore to an alcove where chairs had been set up for the reading. Most of the seats had been claimed, so we made our way to the front, near the lectern.

The room buzzed with conversation. Earlier that day, I'd almost canceled the date with Suzanne. I had labored over my writing, again feeling like I was only masquerading as a writer, and wasn't in the mood for a crowd. But the enthusiastic bustle of the audience energized me and made me glad we'd come.

Kephart did not sequester herself in a back room, like some authors do before readings, but stood at the side of the room waiting to be called forward. After the store manager's introduction, which included a list of accolades, Kephart removed her jacket and found her spot behind the lectern. She greeted us and then explained that her first book had brought her such unexpected attention—it was a National Book Award finalist—that when she sat down to write her second, she'd felt paralyzed. With each book, she'd become more and more sucked into the book writing-marketing-selling world, so much so that she began to feel she was losing her way, was no longer sure what writing meant to her or whether she wanted to continue writing at all.

Hearing that scared me. Though I'm only at the beginning of my writing career, I sometimes wonder whether it is what I want to do forever. What if, despite all my studying and daily writing, I never become a better writer? What if I get bored with it? What if I wake up one day and have nothing left to say?

By the time she'd finished her fourth book, Keph-art said, she felt she'd lost her desire, even her ability, to write. She no longer knew what she wanted to say or what she wanted to do with the rest of her life. As she spoke, she scanned the room, making eye contact with people in the audience, holding her gaze a beat longer than most authors do. Again, I noticed her eyes, glacial blue, recessed in their hollows. After years raising her son—an intense job, as I gathered from A Slant of Sun—now it was time for her to let go, pull back, and nudge him away from her. She wondered whether she should quit writing and work full-time in the business that she and her husband share.

How could someone so gifted think about quitting? I wondered.

She told us she'd had a wonderful time raising her son, but now it was time for her to venture out and find her way too. A couple of years earlier, she'd felt drawn to the gardens of Chanticleer in southeastern Pennsylvania, and so in her "dry spell" she began weekly visits to explore, study, and just be in the Chanticleer gardens.

She opened her book and read the preface to *Ghosts in the Garden*, and I thought I detected the shiver of nerves in her voice. But as she began reading the essays, the strength in her voice took hold, and she held me captivated by the lyricism of her language. Kephart read about a submerged statue she found in the garden, of a woman with outstretched arms, that she called "the drowning girl."

What does it mean to nest a girl so deep inside a pond? To put her there and leave her, so that she might be found again? She reaches, this cast-stone being, with long slender arms. She gathers the minnows to her, but they are independent creatures. She sits and she waits and there is green within her hair—slick patina—for this is what age looks like, in a pond.

Kephart paused, took a sip of water from a glass, and continued.

After I found the girl, I went often to see her, sometimes leaning so far over the pond that my face was floating there beside hers. I took a strange comfort from her eternal peacefulness, the way she simply let the minnows go and refused to fuss about the green in her hair. Escaping words and work, as I was, escaping the knots I had tied my life into, escaping the overwhelming sense that my future was uncertain, I found the girl's easy way with her own circumstances intoxicating. All I had to do was go and let her graces find me.

When she finished reading, Kephart took questions: "Are you a gardener?" "Did you go to the garden with the intention of writing about it?" Kephart said that only now, after her time in the Chanticleer garden and her talks with the gardeners there, is she a gardener. With a sheepish grin, she said that a photograph of her own garden accompanied a recent magazine article and was mistaken by several people for the gardens at Chanticleer.

Then, answering the second question, she turned serious. No, she said, she had not gone to the garden to write about it; she had gone to not write about anything. She took notes about what she witnessed, but had no intention of writing a book. That came later, when she finally understood what it had meant to visit the garden over those two years, understood that words had not left her, that she would still write.

I could have left the reading then; I was completely sated. Suzanne, who hadn't had a chance to eat dinner before the reading, whispered to me, "I came here starving, and now I'm totally filled up."

But we stayed after the reading to have our books signed. It was during my brief exchange with Beth Kephart that she became my latest literary hero— both because of her writing and her way of being.

"I'm a writer," I said, facing her across the signing

table. "And I recently found out that my son has Asperger's."

I surprised myself, by blurting that out. I'd blabbered inane, embarrassing declarations to writers after readings before, and I'd planned to limit myself to, "Would you mind signing your book for me?" or "I loved *A Slant of Sun*; I can't wait to read this one."

I'd gotten brave recently, though, like when I met Zac Unger and told him I loved his memoir about working as an Oakland firefighter, that I also worked in Oakland and he'd really nailed Oakland; the city felt like a character in his book. But another time, I'd sputtered something about my own memoir in progress to a writer after she'd read from her memoir, and it seemed as if she couldn't sign my book fast enough. *Next!* I could hear her thinking as she pushed the book at me and set her eyes on the person behind me.

So when I blurted this out about my son to Beth Kephart, I knew it was because I felt I could, because she'd projected something, made a connection with me, during her reading and the Q & A, that made me know it was all right.

I had also asked the final question: "What do you think you'll do for the next forty years of your life?" She'd spoken several minutes more, her eye contact intense, as if I were the only one there, talking about her good life, her strong marriage, her desire to retain the sense of peace she'd found in the garden. Earlier, when reading an essay about the gardeners she'd befriended, she'd had to wipe away tears, saying, "I don't know why I got so sad reading that."

So possibly all this endeared her to me, made me feel safe telling her this painfully intimate thing about me, even though I was one of many in line eager to have a book signed. I mumbled something about trying to sell my memoir, writing another—this one about my son—and feeling inspired by *A Slant of Sun*. When she spoke she looked only at me, never glancing over my shoulder or hers to see what her friends or her agent were doing, and I felt for a moment like she and I were having coffee and sharing stories about being moms and writers.

"I loved *A Slant of Sun*," I said.

"Jeremy's one hundred percent fine now," she said.

This threw me; I'm not used to writers continuing the conversation their memoir may have started, catching me up on the characters in the story. But it was a wonderful thing for her to say. She was reassuring me, mother to mother.

"How old is he now?" I asked.

"Fifteen," she said. "And I'd always heard that the teen years would be hard."

I had just read that myself, surfing Asperger's Web sites the week before.

"But I'm not finding that true at all," she said. "We're really enjoying him now that he's a teenager."

"It's kind of bumpy for us right now," I said, thinking that "bumpy" didn't begin to describe what we'd been going through. The shouting, rages, time-outs, the tears. "But I hope it'll get better soon."

I wished we were truly having coffee, that we could have finished our conversation, but I was aware of the line behind me. Though she seemed ready to talk for as long as needed, I slid my book toward her and asked, "Would you please sign this for me?"

She took her time inscribing it. We exchanged a few more words and, reluctantly, I moved away.

In the car on the way home, Suzanne and I compared reactions to the reading. "She was so real, wasn't she?" Suzanne asked. "I felt like she was talking just to me."

"I did too," I said.

I didn't read Kephart's inscription until I got home, found my reading glasses, and flipped to the title page. "For Kathy," she had written in the lower right-hand corner. "May your journey—with books and with mothering—bring you peace and fulfillment—Beth Kephart."

I closed the book and placed my glasses on the table. My house was quiet. Her graces had found me.

~Kathy Briccetti

Jump

My dad made manna from the faces of every-day people. "What a nose!" he would quietly gush in restaurants or church pews. "Look at those jowls! Great faces are out today!" He'd take the pencil from behind his ear, flip open his pocket-sized sketchpad, and doodle.

My dad was clearly not like other fathers, swallowed up whole in high-rise office buildings. Spotted fleetingly on trains. Stern and preoccupied with briefcases, suits, hats. He was a cartoonist. His name was Art. It was his job to make the impossible possible. I wanted to be just like him.

Hmm. . . . I'd wonder at random facial features. I'd flip open my notebook, squeeze my number-two pencil, and instead of drawing, I'd write: "Yes, a mouth like an umbrella pinched shut." Ear lobes like tiny violas. The world was a magic hat. You pulled out a rabbit, and it turned into a dove. When you tried to capture its beating heart on paper, the rabbit-dove changed into something else entirely. I was hooked.

My response to the sounds of my hefty grandmother waddling after every meal while chewing Chiclets gum and pinching out an "Eek!" every few footsteps? Write it down. What to do after the red-haired tree outside my bedroom window started flirting with me? Let it flirt in a spiral-bound notebook.

When I burst into Dad's office in the back of our house, excited to share my latest word play, I'd often find him bouncing on his jumpoline, gag cartoon ideas flying up and down with him. Or jogging in place, scanning the newspapers on his desk, fine-tuning the political cartoon ideas that would funnel out to the Chicago suburbs through the *Daily Herald*.

He listened with ears wide open as I rattled my scratchy, off-key descriptions, frequently inspired by Sundays at our cottage on Fox River—hiccupping waves—water skiers gliding through the river like fingers through frosting. Not once did he send me away with a, "Water-skiers aren't fingers, honey. Don't you have anything better to do? Only humans hiccup. Get a grip. Join the real world, will you?"

I knew from the way Dad could take a twenty-minute power nap and wake up with a full-fledged cartoon that we humans saw but a cartoon-bubble's worth of the real world. Moments before Dad's nap, he'd be lightly knocking both sides of his head with his fists, saying, "I got nothing. I got nothing. I need an idea. I'm going to lie down for twenty minutes." Moments afterward, he'd be sitting at his drafting table, his pen hovering over paper in a hurricane of circles. From that storm emerged eyes, bodies, words. "See?" he'd explain. "There's this guy who wants to be a whale. . . ."

Other times, he'd pluck his ideas from the filing cabinet in the back of his head. At least that's what he told my sisters and me. He even drew Mr. Filing Cabinet Head for Chalk Talks. Chalk Talks were the live cartoon-sketching shows he performed for clubs, churches, and private parties. At the end of every show, he'd ask members of the audience to draw a line, any line—a squiggle, a dart, a spiral—and he'd concoct their caricature from it. "The subconscious mind can do anything," he said. "Just think positive."

How wrong our neighbor man was when he whined, "I'd love to just sit around all day drawing pictures." Didn't he get it? This was more than a picture; this was life!

All this cartooning, inventing, what-if-ing was a portal to something mysteriously alive. It was practical, too. It built things. I saw it. Out of Dad's imagination sprang our home, our basement with the Ping-Pong table that conveniently served as a Thanksgiving dinner table and a work table for the cartooning class he taught to neighborhood kids. Imagination created skits and scavenger hunts and stories of my own that people actually published.

"Congratulations!" Dad said, clapping his hands when I published my first poem in *American Girl.* "You're a professional writer now!" (His enthusiasm has spawned two generations of cheerleaders and clap-aholics.) I was eleven, the same age he was when he published his first cartoon. "Don't rest on your laurels," he said when all I wanted to do was gaze at my poem in a magazine. "Now's the time. Send out something else right away. Success breeds success, dear."

After sixteen years of my sending out something else right away, Dad still says that to me. Success does breed success. It also breeds deadlines, revisions, characters, and books that haunt you in the middle of the night.

In his pep talks during my more exasperating moments as a freelance writer, he's kindly revealed some of the muscle behind his magic. Now I know that Mom gratefully grabbed the cash from each of his cartooning students and headed straight for the grocery store. Lost clients and rejections caused Dad to suffer periods of excruciating self-doubt. But when we were cowed with medical bills, he sold to medical magazines. When we needed clothes, he sold to women's magazines. Creative work could be tempestuous, uncertain, and crazy-making. It was also life-making.

Thank God Dad didn't become the second baseman for the Chicago Cubs or a concert pianist as he'd imagined. Thank God his father, with some strange logic, insisted there was no way to make money as a musician, but cartooning, now that was a field you could feed a family on.

Dad is eighty-five years old and still drawing. The last Christmas I flew home to see him, he received an envelope from *Saturday Evening Post*. He fidgeted with it, before finally dropping it in his lap with the rest of his mail. "Should I open it first?" he asked. "No, I'll open it last. No, I'll open it first." Sixty-five years of tearing open envelopes, and the process was just as thrilling. After waving around the two checks in it, he treated the entire family to a holiday feast.

Exuberance and gratitude. Now that's what I call magic. Where's my notebook?

~Jan Henrikson

Of Trifles and Truffles

Here I sit, burrowed into the crowded bedroom I claimed as my writing space when my fourth and final child left home. Insistent sunlight noses its way between the slats of the window blind and pokes inquisitive fingers at the boxes and files that litter my office floor.

My own fingers pluck another frayed envelope from a shoebox full of old love letters—none of them from my husband of thirty-three years. Even now, a full two score and three years later, heat prickles my cheeks as I smooth a dog-eared letter. On second thought, calling it a letter elevates its importance. In reality, I'm staring at nothing more than a boyish scrawl on the brittle page torn from a Big Chief tablet. But the paper, the penmanship—the words themselves—whirl me back to fifth grade and the giddiness of my first serious crush. I can almost smell our budding hormones.

With a lopsided grin, I tuck it away in an archival box, one I label "Childhood."

The stack wedged at my side legitimizes my romantic thoughts. These are from my husband. I pick through printed florist cards, Victorian valentines, silly jottings on the edge of church bulletins, and original poems. Letters dating back to our college years detail our courtship, full of promise and hope. Giggles erupt as, time after time, I encounter, "Dear Sweatheart," a reminder that I married this man of mine in spite of his spelling skills.

I blush as I read suggestive, playful notes from our early married years that plead for together time—away from the kids. I finger recent missives that express the depth and breadth of a more mature love . . . and they nearly take my breath away.

The label for this box: "Marriage."

We're moving, my husband and I, after nearly a quarter of a century in this elastic house that stretched with the arrival of each child and now hangs loose from their departures, slack at the waist. It's time to sort and crate our memories. In the process, I've decided to tackle the piles of paper polluting our home. Snips and bits I've amassed—as every serious writer does—over the span of a lifetime. Here

I sit—surrounded by file folders, cardboard cartons, boxes, and bins—determined to exterminate these pesky invaders. It's a daunting task, one I both relish and rue.

These freeloaders have sneaked into every room of my home. Now I've disturbed their hibernation in the cavernous trunk that once belonged to my grandmother McAdoo. I've pulled them, crinkled, from the back corners of dusty desk drawers. I've discovered them patiently marking my place in an unread novel. These fertile scraps litter my house and reproduce at the same rate as the rabbits my friend Willi breeds for profit. And now here they all sit. Semi-orderly. Patient. As obedient as schoolchildren on the first day of class, waiting to see how the teacher will handle them.

From a bundle bound loosely with florist ribbon, I pull out several cards, letters of condolence sent when my daddy died so unexpectedly eight years ago. It is simple to discard those with only a signature; it is harder to dispose of those that include personal messages. I still feel a profound sense of solace from these heartfelt words of friends who understood my anguish.

With a fine-tipped black marker, I affix another label: "Empathy."

I reach for the teetering twin piles stacked so close to each other they nearly rub shoulders. Clearly, this is a hodgepodge of miscellany. Junk mail and circulars. Editorials and obituaries. Whatever was I thinking when I held on to a community newspaper from Intercourse, Pennsylvania? Sure, the name itself still makes me laugh—as does the incongruity of its Amish roots; yet why did I want to keep it? . . . Ah, I see. This humorous story explains the origin of the village name. And this colloquial one relates the lost history behind shoo-fly pie and divulges a cherished recipe.

What about this Chico catalog? There must have been some reason it didn't land in the recycle bin. I flip through the pages, admiring the store's autumn collection with its figure-flattering separates. The clothes are nice, but . . . I look closer. I read the descriptions. And I remember.

I remember why I squirreled it away several months ago—because of its picturesque words. The catalog brims with a host of unique color names I've never thought to use. There is nothing so mundane as blue, brown, or green in this piece of advertising. Instead, they splash the pages with colors called "commodore," "fudge," and "deep woods." Imagine! But, wait, there's more. Here I find "paprika," "redbay," "rhythm," and "romaine." "Solaria," "gardenia," "Pacific," and "birch."

"Pickle."

"Fireball."

"Chestnut."

"Truffle."

With a new eagerness, I read further and dissect the descriptions. The items listed give the feel of genteel elegance. Of stately, old-family wealth. Why? How? What did they do to achieve this sense of stylish success? Ah, I see. Here is a "eureka necklace," a "champagne scarf," a "Monte Carlo belt." Oh, and "marquis pants." And, listen to this: they use words like "regency," "Vancouver," "Wellesley," "faceted," and "crystal." Phrases like "platinum-studded."

My fingers twitch. My brain races. I actually burn and itch with the sudden desire to write. To create. To taste the words and eat them, to actually roll them around on my tongue and savor their flavor. I want to gorge myself on this catalog and swallow it whole—then regurgitate again and again until I've purged myself of trite phrases, passive sentences, and clichéd metaphor.

I glance around the room of papers I've hoarded. Jottings from my earliest years, messages from acquaintances, epistles from loved ones. They are more than memories, more than relics from my past. They represent a vast array of experiences. They are the collected musings and insights of countless minds. They are a robust conversation that evokes emotion and piques my creativity.

They are my inspiration.

Characters, actions, conflicts, settings, and plots. It's all here. Like an archeologist, I long to dig and uncover. To gather the shards and piece them together. What form will they take? How will I shape them? My mind thrums with possibilities. Oh, the new articles I will fashion, the lyrical poems I will compose, the original stories I will weave.

With a slim blue, er, commodore marker, I write another label, in calligraphy: "Picturesque Writing."

Giving a nod of deep satisfaction, I stack the boxes and set them aside with new resolve. They will accompany me on this move and find a welcome place to settle. In a house with a genuine office, tailored to fit only me. And I know exactly where I'll put them this time: Near my desk. At my fingertips.

~Carol McAdoo Rehme

The Queen of Procrastination

The minutes count down to a satisfying hour or two before my deadline. Now, I can write. The screen blank before me—I love splashing words on it.

It's not the unsoiled page that paralyzes me. All the years of writing news for radio, which will be read seconds later live on the air, have healed that fabulous writers' excuse for not writing. No, I am the queen of procrastination. Procrastination is my ally, my nemesis. I am, perhaps, a secret adrenaline junkie—my only vice.

I am about seven years old when I first declare that I will write a book someday, but first I will have to read Lots of Books to learn how to do it. Well, I overdo it. Lots of Books becomes Thousands of Books. It seems my destiny: first to read voraciously, then to write a book. Even my name holds a clue—at birth, I'd been given the middle name Page.

But for decades I had no voice. After the grace and glamour of living with my romantic, musical, and magical grandparents in New York City my first few years, I am moved miles away and isolated into a terrifying, unpredictable environment ruled by an alcoholic, suicidal mother and a tall, dark, handsome, violent, pedophile stepfather. I am silenced in my childhood by unspeakable events. I literally do not speak in my home, unless words are demanded of me, and I am painfully shy in school. So I read. And many years later, within the safety of my profession, I begin asking questions.

A question I ask Mitch Albom one day in an interview for a national radio show shakes me loose. Albom, who wrote two bestselling books—*Tuesdays with Morrie* and *The Five People You Meet in Heaven*— is chatting with me about his career. We are still taping, and Mitch says he's always wanted to write fiction, but he also felt that he needed to be a journalist first, writing everyone else's story, and then in the second half of his life, he could make it all up. "So," Mitch says, "I look at the calendar, and I say, 'You know, I hate to say it, but you're at the second half.' So I started making it up."

I look up sharply. Mitch's words pierce me, shoot through some hidden tunnel inside me, reverberating at a deep level. I, too, have been a journalist the first half of my life—anchoring and reporting news on radio and television, and for newspapers and magazines. I write news constantly for radio and TV, but my words evaporate into thin air. A couple of my stories end up in anthologies; some book reviews and author interviews land in magazines and online. Ignoring, hiding from the first part of my life, I did not write my truths. No book is in the works.

I draw from Mitch's wisdom, look in the metaphorical mirror. In this instant I know that all those stories I'd locked down inside me are coming out. Time to write my story, to share the wisdom I have acquired that has saved my life, reshaped it, given me joy.

I interview authors. It's my passion and my salvation. Over the last two decades, I've interviewed thousands of authors for a national radio show, the Barnes & Noble Web site, and for book reviews in print and on television. More often than not, when I'm puzzling over a difficult stage in my life or trying to plow through to the next, an author with a book on that very topic will be on tour and want to interview with me. After the interview, still knee to knee, eye to eye,

I would share my personal dilemma and they would share their wisdom on that very slice of life.

When the student is ready, the teacher appears.

That's how I live. The metaphysicians call it Law of Attraction. There's a desire or a dream or a challenge, and I make a wish and let it go, and the answer—the right book—happens to be hand-delivered by the UPS man later that day. At least that's how it appears to me.

I agree wholeheartedly with Albert Einstein, who once said, "There are only two ways to live your life. One is as though nothing is a miracle. The other is as though everything is a miracle." That is why my eyes are open to signs. Author and entrepreneur Squire Rushnell calls such coincidences "God winks." These signs and synchronicities are like an angel tapping you on the shoulder, whispering, "You're on the right path. Hang in there."

So "I'm going to write a book." I say that for two more years. Certainly the intention is set. But apparently I need one more teacher.

I'm driving my silver Mustang convertible around town one day when my cell phone rings. It's the bestselling author of *Fight Club* and numerous other books, Chuck Palahniuk, who lives nearby. He is returning a "hello, how-are-you" message I'd left more than a month prior.

"What are you up to?" Chuck asks.

"Procrastinating writing my book—" And as I open my mouth to punctuate the comment with a giggle, I gasp, "Oh, wow!" instead.

"What?" he asks.

"A white Lexus just came around the corner, with the license plate WRITE—w-r-i-t-e!"

There's a long silence as I await Chuck's next comment.

"Are you in a writers' workshop?" he asks.

"No."

"You are now," Chuck says. "We meet Monday nights."

~Diana Jordan

Learning to Listen

Here I am, working on a perfectly good short-story draft, coming up for a breath of inspirational air, when a new voice begins to whisper in my ear, "Margo's mommy went to the hospital and came home with a new baby boy."

"Shh. Can't you see I'm busy?" I say, trying to sound polite. She sounds awfully young, and I don't want to hurt her feelings. But right now I'm more concerned with what Rachel's going to do when she sees her ex-husband at her daughter's wedding. She's lost seventeen pounds in the past three months and can slither into a size twelve dress; has got these gorgeous acrylic nails, a shade of iridescent coral, courtesy of the Dazzling Nails chain; and bought herself a black dress with a plunging neckline to show off her new shape, not to mention her cleavage. There's no place in the room for a new character's voice, let alone that of a child. I brush the sound away like a pesky fly buzzing around my ear and continue to type.

The bride-to-be walks into her bedroom the morning of the wedding, wearing just a slip of a night-gown, the slightest mound visible through the thin satin covering her lower belly. She is glowing. How does Rachel feel about her daughter's prenuptial pregnancy? She starts to relate how sick she was when she was pregnant, a physical condition her daughter tells her was all in her mind. And then . . .

I lose my way through Rachel's narrative. I cock my head and stare at the words on my computer screen, but no inspiring breezes blow my way. Time to take a break. I head downstairs to the kitchen to fix some lunch.

Here I am, chewing on a perfectly good sandwich, not even thinking about the story, when someone taps me on the shoulder. "Hey, can't you see I'm eating," I say.

A familiar voice, more insistent now, says, "Jenny's mommy went to the hospital and came home with a new baby girl."

"So what?" I ask, a bit more attentive but trying not to show it. This character has got to prove herself. If she can't answer that basic question, she's not worth my time. But my interest is piqued. As a fiction writer,

I'm attuned to threes. She's given me two good opening lines; the third is bound to be a zinger.

"My mommy went to the hospital and had a new
baby girl, but she didn't bring her home," she says.

"How come?" I ask, genuinely concerned.

"'Stillborn,' Mommy calls her."

Okay, she has my attention. I wonder how old this
new character is and if she's an only child. I want to
know her favorite food, who her friends are, and the
toys she likes to play with. Is she quiet and introspec-
tive, or rambunctious and talkative? I have a dozen or
so other questions for her, but I know better than to
quiet her by asking too much too soon. I grab my pen
and a pad of paper. There's just one thing I have to
know before we get started.

"What did you say your name was?" I say, almost
apologetically.

She hesitates a moment. "Lisa," she says.

So now I have a budding character with a compelling voice in an intriguing situation, and I have a
name to assign that voice. I let her begin to lay it all
out for me, how she blamed herself for covering her
ears when Margo's baby cried and holding her nose
when Jenny's baby had her diaper changed. "It isn't
fair," she tells her mother, and her mother agrees. But
when her parents want to name the new baby they

didn't bring home and ask her what she thinks, Lisa closes her eyes and sticks her fingers in her ears.

She tells me more, like about being scared when her mother and father leave the house the first time after they didn't bring the baby home and sneaking a look at the pictures of the little sister she almost had. I listen to the sound of her voice and scribble everything down, like the good writer I am.

Because I am lucky this time, midway through her story I can see how things are going to end up. Lisa does too, but I have a lot more experience in these matters than she does. I've got years of observing how individuals act and react in response to stressful situations, a storehouse of knowledge gleaned from reading and my own personal dealings with people. She's been around for only a couple of hours. It's my job to help her muddle through the middle so that together we can get to that end. Then she'll leave me to tie up the loose story threads and revise her rough verbiage into nice, clean prose.

Hours later, back in my office and deep into this new short-story draft, I realize Rachel has stopped talking to me. She, along with the pregnant bride-to-be, have left the room. For now, I've no idea what happens to them next. Sure, I've been distracted from her story, the one I was originally working on, but one day I'll probably get back to it. After all, I can't leave her out there without resolving the issues she has with her ex-husband. Does she still love him? Does she realize what a cad he really is? But right now, Lisa needs me more.

It's taken me a few years to figure out that each story sets its own timetable, sort of like the Thanksgiving turkey that won't fully cook until it's good and ready, despite what the recipe tells you. I've also discovered that those stories, the ones that find their own voice and come begging to be told, are the most worthy of my telling. All I have to do is stop whatever I'm doing and listen.

~Peggy Duffy

Reading by Flashlight,
Writing by Heart

I'm old enough to remember when chenille was popular the first time around. Or was that the second? The nubby kind. On bedspreads.

As a child of the fifties, I spent many an afternoon nap denuding the chenille bedcover, pulling the tufts as if plucking dandelion heads. Mom was grateful I'd stayed quiet for half an hour, but frowned on the pile of puffs she eventually found under my bed. That was a few short years before Dr. Spock suggested spanking was perhaps not the disciplinary tool of choice.

I am the oldest of five siblings, with only seven years separating the firstborn from the last. Learning to read changed my tolerance for the others. Though I loved them all on some level, they interfered with my life, especially with my ability to read in bed. They tattled.

"Moooom, Cindy's reading again."

"Daaaad, Cindy's light is blinding me."

"Mooom, didn't you say we're s'posed to be sleeping now? Then how come Cindy's not?"

The last sentence often came across sounding like "Cindy snot." Another reason to plan a prison break. So I asked for my own room. And my parents said no.

The two boys shared a room. The three girls shared a room. My parents were keeping their own.

I pointed to the dead-end hallway and asked if I could move my bed there and hang my old, denuded bedspread for a wall and door. They said no a dozen times. Then they rolled their eyes and said yes.

Ah, sweet freedom! I could read by flashlight under the covers well into the night without my sisters ratting me out.

Nancy Drew. The Sugar Creek Gang. The Boxcar Children. Little Women.

Funny that I escaped my real sisters and brothers by reading about other kids' siblings and friends. I never thought about that irony until just now.

Deep affection for my brothers and sisters returned as I matured. My passion for reading intensified too. It carried me relatively unscathed through the emotional tsunami called junior high. Reading soothed me like a literary pacifier and stung me like a cattle prod when I needed it. I'd barely finish one book before thirsting for another.

And now? My book budget far exceeds my clothing

budget. More bookshelves is a permanent request on my Christmas and birthday lists. I still read in bed at night, but long ago gave up the flashlight in favor of a high-intensity halogen light and bifocals.

I write with the same fire that presses me to read. I latch onto a new word with the excitement of a druggie who reaches into his pocket and discovers a packet he forgot was there. I tell myself I can quit anytime, like when company comes. But then I find myself sneaking down to the computer in the middle of the night, because I didn't get my writing fix that day. I can't vacation without at least a pen and pad of paper, and prefer the laptop. I can't leave the house without collecting scene and plot ideas. I can't sit alone in a restaurant without the justifiable eavesdropping I call "characterization research."

Why do I write? An online writers' group to which I belong asked that question a few months ago. I volunteered that for me writing is a collection of magnetic words like those you find plastered on refrigerators. We writers stand in front of the appliance, befuddled by the "without form and void" chaos. Then the Lord places His firm, warm hand over ours and helps us move the words around until they form a clear message. Insight. Hope and healing. Forgiveness and endurance. The promise of spring for the heart's winter.

I write because words have power to change and shape us, to express what seems at first glance inexpressible. I write for the joy of watching a word picture develop like a photograph in a darkroom pan. I write because if the words build up inside me I'll pop a blood vessel. I write because I understand why God created words.

And I write because out there somewhere in the land of magazine and book readers are people like my granddaughter.

Grace surprised her preschool teachers last year by reading whole books without assistance. She devoured books when others her age were still teething on them. She excelled at word recognition so early in the game that we family members entertained ourselves by throwing test words her way to see if it was a fluke or a true gift.

When she came to my house last week to "help" me care for one of my other darling grandbabies, Grace brought a little sack of toys she thought her cousin might enjoy. Among them were two of Grace's current favorite books. Five-year-old Grace plopped Hannah in front of her on the floor and read one of the books to the wide-eyed toddler. When she finished, Grace said to me, "I knew all those words."

"Yes, honey. You did a great job."

"I love to read." This was said with her little hands clasped together and hugged against her chest.

That's my girl.

Then she slipped into philosopher mode and with her bright eyes sparkling and her voice whisper-soft added, "Reading makes my heart have more life in it."

Moments like that are why God invented grandchildren.

And that's why I write.

As I lay my fingers on my ergonomic keyboard, I don't have a Pulitzer or Newberry or RITA or Golden Heart or another award in mind. On the other side of my computer screen sits a reader. Can I pen something that will stir that heart? Will he linger on the final page before closing the cover of one of my books? Will she feel the urge to write a thank-you note, expressing not her praise of me but her gratitude for the experience? Will he catch himself thinking about my characters long after The End?

If I do this right, the reader will sit back in her chair, or nestle into the pillow on her bed where she's been reading by flashlight so as not to disturb her husband, and speak whisper-soft into the night, "Reading makes my heart have more life in it."

~Cynthia Ruchti

23½ Love Letters

I raised my knuckles to rap on the apartment door, but then glanced at my watch. Five minutes early for my blind date. I lowered my hand and considered backing out.

After rehearsing various excuses I could deliver over the phone, I thought about returning to my dreary apartment, the easy chair with a reading lamp and a stack of novels beside it, and the large photo collage of gorgeous women friends, not a lover among them. Still, I wrote to them regularly since my move from Maryland to South Carolina. I didn't consider myself a real writer, because I didn't take much pleasure in the process. And I apparently wasn't a good writer, because my entreaties had never compelled any of those women to reply with a simple, declarative "Yes."

My friend Adra, another beauty who liked me only as a friend, had arranged the blind date with her best pal, Kate. For the first time in years, I was due to have dinner with a woman who had not yet pigeonholed me. If I didn't cut and run.

Thinking about the latest batch of letters on my table and the probability that my responses to them would score only more platonic points, I knocked on Kate's door. Hard.

She opened it so fast she must've been standing on the other side, watching my deliberation through the peephole. Her red hair and bright green eyes made me think of Christmas. She was lovely, just as Adra had promised, and a lively intellect blazed there too. I recognized it instantly—every woman depicted on my wall possessed a similar spark. All too easily, I could see her among them, another Dorothy Parker to correspond with and nothing more.

I extended my hand and introduced myself, hoping that I didn't betray my declining expectations.

"I'm Kate McDonald," she said. Her handshake felt confident. She pivoted away from the door and invited me inside with a small, graceful bow. I watched her skirt swirl as she glided on strong, slim legs. Her dress shoes barely made a sound on the hardwood floor. Adra had mentioned that Kate used to be a ballet dancer. Prompted by a stubborn romantic streak, words describing her elegance leapt into my mind.

At the same time, the cynic in me was already writing the all-too-familiar end to the story.

My friend Adra was already there and stood as Kate and I entered the room. She introduced me to her boyfriend, Richard. He drove the three of us to a nearby bistro, all the while telling funny stories about being a transplant from the North. Kate sat beside me in the backseat. Every time I asked her a question, Richard would launch into his next anecdote. She finally shrugged at me, and we gave up trying to talk.

In the restaurant, Adra tried to rein in Richard, but I found him fascinating. I had only to toss out a topic, like dropping a coin in a jukebox, and he spun another great tale. Besides, there wasn't any real magic with Kate, just friendly camaraderie. I recognized the direction our evening was taking. The only question was, would I bother trying to garner one more friend?

Adra suggested at the end of the meal that we go for a walk, since recent showers had cooled the brutal July weather. Following the path along the Savannah River, Adra pulled Richard aside, and Kate and I proceeded ahead of them.

I glanced around, realizing that I couldn't hear the other man for the first time since entering Kate's living room. She seemed to float beside me, lovely and graceful even against the background of brown water sloshing against the shore. I asked, "What do you like to do for fun?"

"I've always loved to read."

We compared favorite authors, and I found her tastes much more literary than my own. Afraid of appearing lowbrow, I changed subjects. "Do you miss dancing in the ballet?"

"No, remembering all of those steps was too hard for me. With books, a bad memory is an advantage: I can re-read one and enjoy it as much as the first time." She glanced at me while I laughed. "Do you like to dance?"

"I have a good memory, but no sense of balance."

Kate said, "We can do something about that." She led me to a playground nearby. Beyond the swing set and jungle gym sat a teeterboard, a large wooden square with a six-inch pole underneath its center to hold it in the ground and keep it forever lopsided.

"Climb on," she commanded. Kate stood on one end, and then I chose an edge beside her, which sent her nimbly prancing toward me. She hopped to the opposite side, and the board tilted again, causing me to stumble while I tried to recover my footing. Even holding on to her arms, I found it impossible to retain any equilibrium. I felt like a kid again as we eased around the board, creating fresh chaos with each step.

We laughed so hard that we couldn't hear Richard talking as he approached with Adra.

Despite Kate's promise of improved balance, I staggered beside her like a drunken sailor on the way back to the car. She didn't seem to mind holding me upright. If Richard resumed his stories during our return to Kate's place, I missed them as she and I continued to amuse each other. I forgot all about that cynic who'd already written the epitaph on our relationship.

We made lunch plans for the next day and reluctantly said goodnight. All the way home I sang at the top of my lungs and from the bottom of my heart. However, when I entered my apartment, her voice on my answering machine greeted me. "While we were out, my boss called with a new auditing assignment. I have to fly to San Francisco in the morning. I'll be gone for a few weeks with lots of late nights, but we can still play phone tag like this. Sorry about lunch. I had fun tonight—you give a good teeter."

I wrote down the hotel phone number she left and stared at the collage of women friends. After so many chances thwarted or missed, what was one more?

At four in the morning, gazing at the ceiling, I knew Kate was different from the others. I could not allow her to be just another beautiful face on my wall. She would be in my life for good or out of it forever.

I gave up trying to sleep as I gave in to my emotions. I called the hotel in San Francisco and requested the street address. Kate deserved more than a message slip or a tinny thirty-second monologue. I wanted to send her letters that would change both our lives.

Although I always enjoyed composition, I was never a fan of rewriting. As a teenager I'd scribbled a number of first-draft stories that I filed away, never daring to invite critique. In school, low teacher expectations and my ability to string credible sentences together on my initial attempt produced good grades and very little threat to my ego. And for my cadre of gorgeous pen-pals, I could fill entire pages with glib observations and double-entendres without having to reconsider a single quip.

I called in sick to work so I could focus on writing to Kate. Instead of making real progress, though, I found myself scrapping countless false starts. Nothing was coming out as well as she deserved. Instead of hiding behind humor, I'd decided for once to express myself honestly, but summoning each perfect word was like trying to pass a chain of kidney stones. The morning and afternoon rushed by, and suddenly I had less than an hour to finish my first true love letter and rush to the post office so Kate could receive it the next day.

As soon as I sealed the Express Mail envelope and handed it to the clerk, I felt certain that everything I'd written was wrong. Worse, it was insipid and stupid. The thought of waiting days for her disappointed reply sent me back to my writing desk again. By late evening, I had another letter ready to go, this one trying to rectify the damage I thought I'd done. I didn't back away from my initial sentiments; I just tried to state them more clearly.

My passion for her seemed to have rekindled my passion for writing. I even pulled out my old stories and glanced through them. A couple of ideas were worth keeping. After extensive reworking, maybe I'd even show them to Kate, if my letters hadn't scared her off.

Receiving her first reply eclipsed all the excitement and anxiety of writing to her. I held the envelope for long moments, wondering what it held—the lady or the tiger. I discovered the lady inside, but one who wrote with far more poetry, wit, and intelligence than my letters conveyed. She further distinguished her prose with exquisite calligraphy. The tiger came from within me, shredding my nascent writer's ego with claws and fangs.

In a moment of masochism, I reread Kate's letter. Only then did I realize that while she didn't echo my sentiments, neither did she discourage my pursuit.

I even sensed a tentative approval to proceed, and hoped I hadn't become delusional.

Our correspondence continued apace, with Kate remaining cautious. I took this as a challenge to express myself better. My writing evolved as I learned what she responded to best. By trusting the process of rewriting to lead me there, I could craft letters as precise and unambiguous as prisms; the words glowed like suns on the page and would cast bright, pure colors over her heart as she read.

We made a date for the evening after she'd returned—dinner at my place. I put the photos of my friends away, praying that my days of longing had ended. After our meal, I showed her the best short story I'd written, about a man who could be a perfect mate but feared risking hurt and rejection.

Kate read it through to the end and looked at me. "Arc you a good kisser?"

Taking this as approval of my work, I stammered, "I think so."

"Show me."

Soon she had to travel again, so we resumed writing our letters, but with more intimacy and momentum. In October, reunited once more, I asked the shortest question I ever posed to Kate: just four words. She replied with one syllable and, to my overwhelming joy, three letters instead of two.

We wrote our wedding vows by excerpting our letters, including the most recent one I'd started. Adra, the one who'd made it all possible, was the first to receive an invitation to the ceremony. One month after the wedding, with Kate on the road, I resumed my twenty-fourth love letter.

Over the years, she encouraged me to take writing courses and join writers' clubs and critique groups. The more I wrote, the more I wanted to write. A decade after our wedding, Kate told me to quit my job and write full time. Because of her, I fill my days with the building blocks of words, the blueprints of characters, and the architecture of stories.

Because of her, I am a writer.

~*George Weinstein*

Raw Material

I t must be difficult, being related to me. Or being related to any writer. It must be disconcerting to see a part of you dissected in print, your privacy invaded, or to notice vestiges of yourself in fictional characters. Once I wrote a short story with an insensitive, workaholic husband in it. "Am I that bad?" my husband asked me. I reassured him that it was, in fact, fiction. The character may have shared certain qualities with my husband, his hands or his affinity for his bicycle, but the accompanying flaws, purely fictional, served the story.

My husband and I recently saw the movie *Something's Gotta Give*, in which Diane Keaton portrays a well-regarded playwright. Jack Nicholson's character, Harry, is discomfited to find scenes, almost verbatim, from their past relationship in her new play. He feels exposed and embarrassed. But it's not really him, the writer explains; the character in the play is named Henry, not Harry. Besides, Henry is killed off in act two, which doesn't exactly set his mind at ease. I believe my husband found much with which to identify in that scene of the film.

With nonfiction, the real-life subjects have nowhere to hide. My daughters have grown up with a mother who speculates and muses about them publicly, and while they may think this is normal, it is something about which I am sometimes seized with guilt. I worry that I have shamelessly exploited our family experiences for the sake of a deadline. I worry that my loved ones appear in print more frequently than they might appreciate. But once, while visiting one of my daughters in her college dorm, I was surprised and delighted to see one of my columns posted on her door. So perhaps they will not be scarred for life.

Once I wrote an essay about my childhood that offended my mother. She thought I had invented an episode that cast a negative light on her. We argued over the condition of my long-term memory. I insisted my version was correct and served to illustrate a larger point. In the end, she said she was just glad the essay had been printed in a newspaper, where it would be forgotten in no time and end up, to quote her, "wrapping fish."

Although her statement cut deep, she was right. My words were ephemeral, as flimsy as the paper on

which they were printed. They would be read by who-
ever had time that morning over coffee or that evening in the recliner, and then discarded. Newspapers
are delivered, read or browsed, and piled up until they
go on to ignoble, secondary uses. My essay would
indeed be forgotten. It would wrap fish.

The implication I struggled with was that that
was all my work was good for.

Over the years I have gotten used to the business involved in sharing my soul. At first, the heart
and fire in my essays seemed lacking when typed and
set by someone else. The words had a cold, alien
quality on paper, or worse, they became a pedestrian
read. And editors, working for clarity or space, often
removed an inspired image or an essential adjective.
Their cosmetic surgery, the calm slicing of a mole, to
me was more akin to amputating a limb.

Hardest to accept, my published work did not
change the world. It did not enlighten the masses, did
not turn bad hearts good, did not open closed minds,
did not make me an authority. Every now and then a
kind friend would clip something for the fridge mag-
nets or a stranger would call to thank me. The recognition tasted good, but it was gravy, not sustenance.

I was sorry that particular essay hurt my mother's
feelings, but I knew that it was a strong, honest piece.
I also knew that as a writer, if I started to censor myself

for expressions that might upset someone, I could not write. My life, and all that has touched it, is the raw material in my work. It is the soil and the seed for my produce. With words, I only add water and keep it in a sunny spot until fruition. So my intent in writing is not offense, it is growth. That's my best apology.

If my words, once printed, are then read by someone, the connection is complete, from writer to reader, from me to you. I can ask no more. Then, if my newsprint words catch a child's paint spills, or guard the family china in a move, or provide a bed to a new puppy, or wrap fish, so be it. Newspaper is supposed to be recycled, just as writers recycle thoughts, emotions, impressions, and words.

~Valerie Schultz

This story was first published in the *Bakersfield Californian*, March 22, 2004.

Lament of the Aspiring Writer

D o I need to chain you to your writing desk?"
I pulled my head out from underneath the
pillow just enough to squinch one eye at my husband.
Yep. He looked like he meant it.

I couldn't blame him for being frustrated. I was
having one of my "artistic fits of pique." As poetic as
they sound, these episodes are nothing more than me
throwing myself onto the bed and wailing, "Whatever
made me think I could be a writer? This is stupid—
I'm just wasting my time. . . . Sob, sob, sniffle, sniffle.
. . . Maybe I should just give up and go get a real job."
Now, I don't know what this terrifying "real job" is,
but I know it's horrible and I don't want anything to
do with it. I'd much rather be writing.

"Seriously, honey, you need to get a grip," he said,
putting on his work uniform. My artistic funks usually
hit at about the same time he needs to get ready for

work. "You've wanted this your whole life. Why are you torturing yourself over it now?"

"Because I'm wasting my time," I wailed, sitting up. "This is ridiculous. Do you know how hard it is to get published? All the how-to books—."

He held up his hand to silence me. "Forget the how-to books. If everyone listened to the naysayers of the world, nothing great would ever get accomplished. I hear about people beating the odds all the time."

"And that's why you hear about them, because it's so rare to beat the odds."

He sighed. "So why can't you be one of the people who beats the odds?"

"Because I can't get anything written, much less sent out to a publisher." I lowered my voice to whisper the most horrible words a writer can utter. "I have writer's block."

He laughed and shook his head.

I sighed. He just didn't understand, and I really didn't want to talk about it anyway.

For almost twenty years, I'd fantasized about the day I could devote myself full-time to my dream of writing. And there I was, drawing near to the end of my first year as a dedicated writer, and I had only two stories out making the rounds and a third story almost ready. I had four novels started, but each was only about ten thousand words long. I'd been waiting twenty years for this?

"You don't have writer's block. You just spend way too much time doing everything but writing. You've wanted to write for as long as I've known you, and now you have your chance. But you spend all your time thinking about writing and very little time actually writing." He grabbed his watch off the nightstand and opened the bedroom door. He stepped out the door, then paused and turned to look back at me. "How much time did you spend writing yesterday?"

"All day." I hoped I sounded convincing.

"Yeah, right."

I opened my mouth to protest but he held up his hand again and gave me a sad smile. "Honey, I know you can do this. Just sit down, shut up, and write. It's that simple." He shrugged and disappeared out the door.

I sat on the bed and pouted. Easy for him to say; he didn't have a million other things to take care of. I really wanted to write, but other things always seemed to get in the way. In spite of all my good intentions, yesterday had turned out like every other day that whole year.

I sat down at my desk and fired up my computer. While I waited for the computer to boot up, I made sure all my pens were in a neat row, near at hand.

Then I opened my word-processing program to the daily writing prompt.

"Okay, today's prompt: write about a childhood memory." I nodded. I can do that. I sat back in my chair and rubbed my chin. "Okay, think of a childhood memory . . . a childhood memory." I heard a soft scraping noise begin in the kitchen, like someone trying to sandpaper a teeny-tiny block of wood. I tried to ignore it, but the repetitive *scritch-scritch* began to drill into my brain. That noise was not going to be ignored. I stomped into the kitchen and found three cats grazing in the stack of dirty dishes. "Whatever," I muttered, and waved my hand. "Let them graze until I get some writing done." One of the cats took my dismissive wave as some kind of threat and ran. A bowl by his side wobbled, and I held my breath, waiting for it to clatter to the floor. It didn't, but I took the hint. "Fine! I'll load the dishwasher real quick and then get back to writing."

I cleared off the counters and ran into another problem: The dishwasher wasn't quite full. But I knew the refrigerator had at least two weeks of leftovers in it, so I could get a full load if I cleaned out the fridge and put the storage dishes in the dishwasher.

Halfway through emptying the fridge, the kitchen garbage filled. So I stopped and ran it out to the main can and put a new bag in the kitchen can. I returned to emptying the fridge and spilled old spaghetti sauce all over my PJs (because I was still in my PJs, of course; I am, after all, a writer). So I had to change, and I needed to treat the stain before it set in, because those were my favorite pajamas. Not to mention I only have one other pair of pajamas, anyway, since my clothing budget is so tight (I am, after all, a writer). Then I thought I might as well throw the stained clothes in the laundry while I was at it. While gathering up a load to go with the PJs, I noticed the hamper was pretty full, so I decided I'd better stay on top of that and get at least a few loads of laundry done.

I got the laundry on and went back to filling the dishwasher. But a new problem arose: Emptying the fridge led to more than one load of dishes. I made a mental note to listen for the end of the dishwasher cycle so I could get the next dishwasher load going right away. Now I needed to keep one ear peeled for the dishwasher and the other peeled for the washing machine. Fine. I didn't need my ears to write.

I grabbed myself a quick drink from the fridge before getting back to writing and noticed that I was out of milk. I couldn't make supper without milk. I sighed. Now I had to stop and make myself presentable—just because I write horror doesn't mean I have to look scary—and run to the store for some milk.

As I passed through the hallway on my way to the bathroom to get ready, I had to stop and clean up a hairball some digestively distressed cat had urped up on the carpet. (That'll teach him to graze in the dirty dishes.) I went back to the kitchen to throw away the used paper towels and found the dog sitting by the back door, giving me the "my eyeballs are floating" look. I took the dog out to go potty—a twenty-minute task, since, in her opinion, peeing is an exact science; every pee has its perfect spot, and to put it in any spot other than its perfect spot would cause the Earth to fall out of orbit. Then I finished getting ready and headed for the grocery store.

Two hours and six bags of groceries later, I returned home to write. But by then it was time to make supper. And the laundry was done and ready for the next load, and the dishwasher was done and ready for the next load, and the water heater thermostat had kicked out and needed to be reset (thanks to running the dishwasher and the washing machine at the same time), and I noticed the fence gate was squeaky when I came in. . . .

And by the time it was all done, I was just too tired to write. And so it was that yesterday had passed without a single word written.

I thought about what my husband had said, and realized I had fallen into the same trap so many other aspiring writers do: I was spending too much time aspiring to write and very little time actually writing. Even though I finally had time to pursue my dream, I was still making it a low priority in my life. I was talking the talk, but wasn't writing the write.

I sat down at the computer a writer reborn. I set a goal of one thousand words a day, and I wasn't going to move from that chair until the goal was met, no matter what. I did spend a little time that first day spinning around in the chair, trying to balance a pencil on my upper lip. But then a funny thing happened: Inspiration struck, and I began to write. When hubby came home for lunch, I was still busily typing away at my computer. Sure, the dog threw herself at him in her joy at seeing someone who would take her outside to find "the perfect spot," but I was actually writing!

I did the same thing the next day, and the next day, and the day after that. After six months, I had thirteen short stories making the rounds, a novel in the revision stage, and two works accepted for publication. It's not much, but it is a start—and it's a huge improvement over the whole previous year. And all I did was "sit down, shut up, and write!" That's how the dream becomes reality and the aspiring writer becomes a writer.

~Brenda Kezar

On Unconditional Love
and Rejection Slips

The grapefruit squirted me in the eye, making it burn and tear up. Just then my grandmother came into the dining room with the mail and placed it by my mother, who scanned the voluminous pile before pulling out one envelope. She eyed the thin envelope rather cautiously, paused, and then took it and the other mail and tossed them into the waste-paper basket. My grandmother watched silently, but not for long.

"Really! You can at least open it and read it," she said.

"I don't want to see one more rejection slip. Period!" my mother answered.

"Poor Mommy," I said. "Don't feel bad. You're a good writer." But the words of a ten-year-old, while appreciated, were lost in the thick air of adult tension that filled the room.

"Well, I'm going to open it," my grandmother said.

"Just leave it!" my mother commanded.

Drama at high noon on a Saturday. I straightened and sat forward, anticipating the eruption soon to come.

My grandmother fully ignored my mother, took the wastebasket—which my mother attempted to grab from her—held it tightly to her chest, and walked out of the room. I watched, transfixed, as my mother seethed.

My father could never understand the relationship between his wife and mother-in-law. Though long divorced from my mother, he would often later recall the times my mother and grandmother would fight, their voices reaching a high pitch and rage burning in their eyes. Each would go off in a different direction, slamming doors behind them. He would think, *That's it. They'll never talk again. This time it's over. What a shame*—only to be surprised when, ten minutes later, they would be talking and laughing, as though no fight had ever occurred. It never ceased to amaze him. Poor Father. Poor people who have never known the security and joy of unconditional love.

So I wasn't worried about their squabble over the mail that day. I knew my mother and grandmother would make up. First, though, a tug-of-war between these two souls would have to occur.

My grandmother searched through the basket, mumbling under her breath. My mother ignored her, deliberately not watching, her face filled with fury. Growing frustrated with not finding what she was looking for, my grandmother suddenly turned the basket over and let the letters fall all over the floor. She bent down, appearing to me somehow older and more vulnerable than her character displayed, and pulled out the envelope in question. She looked up, shook her head, and tore open the letter. I was mute. My grandmother stood there, reading the letter silently, saying nothing. My mother poked at her food like the sulking child my grandmother had, perhaps, momentarily reduced her to. My heart was racing with anticipation. What a fight this would be! I was becoming uncomfortable at the thought.

My grandmother finished reading the letter and, in a rather unique fashion, straightened up and charged into the room. "There," she said, shoving the letter under my mother's nose, moving her brunch aside, and jabbing the letter with her finger. "There!"

"Please, Mother," my mother said, pushing the letter away from her.

"Read it!" my grandmother said, pushing it back.

"Leave me alone. I'm not going to read it," my mother said.

"It's an acceptance!" my grandmother said.

My mother stopped. She looked first at me, then at my grandmother. She eyed her mother carefully to be sure this was real. My grandmother waited. Slowly, my mother read the words: "We are happy to inform you. . . ." I watched as her face turned from disbelief to joy. I sat in awe.

My grandmother acquired a victorious air about her, though I'm certain she, too, was shocked by the unexpected good news. I would say she had scored a double victory: She had witnessed her daughter's discouragement turn to joy, and to her delight (she couldn't help it), she had maintained her reign as the mother who, thus far undefeated, knew best. She wore a caricature pleased-as-punch look on her face.

My mother jumped up and hugged my grandmother, who was now glowing. And I, caught up in the emotion, jumped up and hugged them both.

I sit at the breakfast table now and open my letters cautiously, looking to see whether the mail will bring me a rejection slip. When it comes, it is often my son who buoys me. "Don't worry, Mommy. You're a good writer. The editor's stupid." I have him well trained.

But there are times when I open the mail alone,

knowing all too well that the editors aren't stupid and worrying that maybe I'm not good enough. And there are times when I take the mail, unopened, and begin to reach for the garbage. It is then that the memory comes back at its sharpest and most acute. I see my mother and my grandmother. I feel the sting of the grapefruit. I remember the stony silence while my grandmother sifts through the basket. I remember the tearful joy of these two people I loved as they held each other. I think of the mother who died far too young and of the grandmother who then reached to me, as I did to her.

After the pain that accompanies memories of people long gone subsides, I think how writing is a part of me—its frustrations and its joys. It requires both perseverance and belief. I am able to feel my mother and grandmother reach for the basket, shaking their heads at me, urging me to open the letter. And it no longer matters whether the mail holds an acceptance or a rejection, for I have learned about unconditional love.

~Pat Gallant

The Voice in My Head

The classroom was very still. Twenty-five kids listened raptly as I read my short story aloud in my high school creative writing class. My hands shook, and I could hardly breathe. The assignment was not difficult, and I wondered why my teacher had chosen my story, above twenty-five others, to be read to the class.

When I finished, the class applauded. Then the teacher asked if anyone had any comments or questions. Most of the comments were complimentary. They were absorbed; they found the story fun or interesting; they thought the writing was good. There was only one negative comment, which came from a boy I had a secret crush on. He said it was not original enough, that it sounded like a copy. When asked, he couldn't say what he thought it was a copy of. But that didn't register with me. Nor that mine was the story the teacher had selected as the best. Nor that everyone else in the class liked it. What I latched on to was that one person in the whole class didn't like it. It was his comment, above all, that stayed with me. And it crushed me.

For that entire term, maybe for years afterward, maybe for my entire life, there was a nagging voice in my head whenever I wrote something. "It isn't original enough. I am not a good writer."

When I graduated from high school, my creative writing teacher wrote in my yearbook, "A little too silent, but always profound." I have never forgotten that. But I never believed it.

My professional career was not as a writer. I was a dancer, an actress, a literary agent, a theater manager, a producer of plays and films. But I always wrote. When I was a dancer I wrote articles in dance magazines. I wrote plays for fundraising events for hospitals and schools. I was on the research/writing team of a documentary television series. But I never considered myself a writer. I didn't think I was good enough. That voice was always in my head.

When I was a working dancer/actress in Los Angeles, I wrote a pilot for a television series and sent it to one producer. He eventually wrote back, saying they were not interested. A few years later, a new television series came out that was clearly based on my idea—the pilot was almost exactly as I had written it.

But the fact is, I hadn't written it. They stole my idea, but my writing wasn't good enough, I told myself.

When I decided to produce films, I wrote two short screenplays for my burgeoning film company. The first was accepted by a not-for-profit organization as a fundraising tool; the second won awards in film festivals. Not for the writing, I told myself. Not because the writing was good.

I wrote a book for tween-agers—young girls from ten to thirteen years of age. I actually found an agent for it, who sent it out to about ten publishers, all rejects. Alas, the agent died and nobody else at the agency wanted to take it on. I gave it to a friend of mine to read—someone whom I respected immensely, a high school teacher of English and literature. She told me it read a little too old-fashioned. Too British, in a way. It had too many big words and images. Young kids wouldn't like it. In other words, in my mind, it wasn't original enough.

I didn't look for another agent. It didn't matter, I wasn't really a writer.

That was before the Harry Potter series. My book, too, was a fantasy. I reread the rejection letters. They were more complimentary than most acceptance letters I had seen, but the publishers didn't know what to do with it. I realized I had never really read those letters. All I saw was "rejected."

Then one day I saw a notice on the Internet that A *Cup of Comfort*® was looking for short stories about real people who were—or had done something—beyond the ordinary. And I thought, "I can do that." So without hesitation I wrote something. And then promptly forgot about it. I did it only for the fun of it. Because I enjoyed writing. I expected nothing.

When my story was accepted, I was shocked. And elated! Maybe I am good enough.

Since then I have written two full-length screenplays that I will be producing and that have been critically praised. I have picked up my old children's book and gotten some very positive feedback and encouragement from a group of professional children's book authors. And I am beginning to feel, at a relatively advanced age, that maybe what I am going to be from now on is a Writer—with a capital W.

Now, when other writers give me something of theirs to read, I encourage them. Writers can be very thin-skinned, and one negative voice can stop them in their path. I don't want that voice to be mine. Besides, if someone really wants to write, it doesn't matter what I believe. What's important is that they want to write. And so I say to them the same thing I now say to the voice in my head. Right on! Write on.

~Gila Zalon

Writing without Pizza

Being fat had its obvious rewards. Writing with an open box of Sugar Pops next to my thick thigh had always been a comfort. When I lacked ideas, chewing on a mouthful of pretzels helped stimulate my brain. A Dairy Queen Blizzard or an Entenmann's pound cake helped steady my nerves when I became anxious about exceeding a word count. Food helped me write. Food helped me be funny. But when the scale topped 225 pounds and my doctor started screaming things at me about killing myself bite by bite—with every super-sized order of fries and every pizza I inhaled by myself—I knew it was time to repair my body. Who would have known that as an unexpected side effect, I'd put a little spice in my creative spirit?

On a rampage, I started throwing out all the food in my house. That is how I always address things; for me, it's all or nothing. I was going to lick this thing, and that meant putting an end to the licking, as well as the chewing and swallowing, of anything and everything my taste buds desired. No more fattening food. No more in-between-meal snacks. No more munching while I typed through the night. If I was going to see success, I had to get back in control.

What was odd about my weight gain was that I had always been so in control of every other aspect of my life. I was organized and ambitious. Being out of control in my eating habits was out of character. In addition to my "real" job as an educational therapist and my unpaid volunteer work at MomCanYouRight-NowINeedItYesterday, I was able to pump out more writing than some full-time authors. I was just out of control with my eating habits and physical fitness.

The truth is, and this may be hard for a person who has never had a weight problem to comprehend, I just didn't see it. My creative imagination was both a blessing and a curse. I would see skinny staring back at me in the mirror, when what was really there was an overweight, large, and sloppy body on my five foot, two inch frame. I saw sexy when the mirror was really reflecting a jumbo-sized walking meatball. I had convinced myself and had even sold articles about how sizing of garments in America has changed over the last twenty years.

Yet, I became determined—for the first time since six months before my wedding day twenty-five years earlier (which had something to do with buying an expensive dress that was too small in the first place)—to be the healthiest-looking kid on the block. I read and researched, and I became the obnoxious resident expert on protein, carbohydrates, fat, and all aspects of vitamins and nutrition. When the scale showed that I had lost seventy pounds, I even told one second-grade ADHD student I work with that, in weight, I had lost two of her! She didn't understand, but that was irrelevant.

As for its effect on my writing, dieting has had its ups and downs (pun intended). At first, sans Milky Ways, Milk Duds, and Whoppers, I couldn't write. I had convinced myself that there was nothing stimulating in vegetables disguised as finger foods. A writer needed fist foods! Nibbling was for people who write with pens or have time for manicures; broken-nailed computer authors needed to gulp, chomp, and burp their way to each deadline. Before the diet, a creative break was a visit to inspect the inside of my refrigerator. A post-fatty writing break has become swimming fifty laps in my pool or a brisk walk through suburbia.

Weight loss has brought a new category to my resume of writing credits. I now write about health, dieting, and nutrition. I have also read enough good information and asked enough experts specific questions during my own weight-loss quest to make me extremely well informed. I also know firsthand about the struggles and difficulties that come with both being overweight and with losing large quantities of weight, and I can relate to the joy of fitting into junior-sized capri pants. The best part is that I can approach this with wit and wisdom, and I can share this with others who are where I used to be.

To date, besides losing weight, I have gained five new clips and a new selection of places to submit my work. That's not to say I still don't dream in shades of hot fudge, but, as a writer, losing has become winning when those checks from new markets arrive.

~Felice Prager

This story was first published in *Writer's Weekly* e-zine, November 2, 2005.

The Inklets

Almost everyone is writing, or thinking about writing, the Great American Novel. Today, nearly anyone with a computer and printer considers himself to be a writer. If you don't believe me, just ask an editor . . . any editor. On second thought, don't bother. Most of them are too busy being inundated with submissions from writers who are convinced they have authored The Next Bestseller.

The only thing more prevalent than writers is advice for writers. "Write what you know." "Write something—anything—every day." "Show, don't tell." "Be thorough in your research." "Know your audience." "Join a writers' critique group."

J. R. R. Tolkien and C. S. Lewis had The Inklings. I have The Inklets.

Writing can be a lonely occupation. Just me and the computer. Sometimes the words flow faster than

I can type. More often, I'm staring at a blank screen and a blinking cursor. Lonely, maybe, but I'm not alone.

The Inklings were an all-male literary group that met weekly, on Thursday nights, in the 1930s and 1940s. Members included prominent literary figures of the time, many of whom were associated with Oxford University: Tolkien, Lewis, Charles Williams, Owen Barfield, John Wain, and others. Meetings included reading and critiquing each other's work.

The Inklets is an all-female writers' critique group. We also meet weekly, on Thursday nights, to give and receive candid feedback about our work. That work might consist of a single paragraph or a chapter, depending on how active our Muse has been. Our meetings started out in the local library and have since moved to each other's homes. In between, we've met in restaurants and parks. But it's not about the location, it's about the members.

Four women, in various seasons of life—married with grown children, single without children, married with no children. Some of us are employed in full-time careers; others are retired. Our writing styles are as different as our lives and personalities. One special-izes in mystery romance, another in short stories; one's passion is faith-based writing, while the fourth writes dramatic literary fiction. But we have a single common bond: our love for the written word. Parodying a popular advertising campaign, our motto is, "Got words?"

The Inklets are the ones to whom I bare my soul when I reveal what I have carefully crafted on the page. They, in turn, comment on everything from grammar and punctuation to style, voice, and vocabulary. Of course, being a member of this group isn't always easy. Participating in a critique group has been likened to showing someone your beautiful baby and having them tell you how ugly he is. It takes a thick skin to listen to others comment on my work . . .

"Good description, but your run-on sentences are exhausting to read."

"Nice, concise writing, but where's the emotion?"

"Love the emotion, but your choice of adjectives is lazy. Be more creative."

"Compelling plot, but the characters need more development."

"Excellent character development, but where's the conflict?"

"Great action, but your POV jumps back and forth."

It's the "but" that gets me every time. Still, their feedback helps me to refine my writing, to make it the best it can be. I'd much rather receive their critiques than have an editor reject my work for weaknesses that could have been corrected prior to submission.

Then again, it's not always about the critique. Sometimes it's just about talking to someone who understands the roller-coaster nature of the creative process . . .

"I've stared at a blank page all week. Nothing's coming."

"My heroine's ex-husband isn't listening to me. I thought he was dead in chapter one, but he's not cooperating."

"I was in the middle of a steamy love scene when my husband asked if dinner was ready."

"The dialogue in this chapter was more like taking dictation than writing."

"I thought I knew where this story was going, but I haven't had a new idea in weeks."

"My two main characters played out an entire scene in my head yesterday, but I was in line at the supermarket and I couldn't write it down."

Sometimes we share writing tips . . .

"I found a great Web site for help with query letters and book proposals."

"A Cup of Comfort® is looking for submissions."

"Did you know Strunk's Elements of Style is online?"

"The bookstore is sponsoring a writing contest for the best mystery-solving hero."

"There's a regional writers' conference in March. Who wants to carpool?"

And sometimes it's not about the writing at all. Sometimes it's just about support . . .

"I'm moving Saturday. Anyone have a truck I can use?"

"Another rejection. At this rate I'll have enough rejection letters to wallpaper the bedroom."

"I'm having surgery in two weeks."

"My son is back in town. I miss my empty nest."

"I've got a book signing next month. You'll be there for moral support, right?"

One of our members put it best:

"The Thursday night meeting of The Inklets, also known in lighter moments as The Chicklets, will meet at five-thirty. Minutes of the last meeting will not be read, as no one can write as fast as The Inklets can talk. The meeting will be called to order, but will be disorderly. The meeting will be dismissed when it is over."

And yes, The Inklets have critiqued this with a careful eye.

~Ava Pennington

Flow

I spent the month of January at Soapstone, a writing retreat for women on the Oregon coast. Soapstone is a nonprofit organization that houses two women at a time in a creekside cabin in the forest.

As I was preparing for my month of intensely focused writing, I learned that very few people appreciate that unpaid work is, nonetheless, still work. The concept of a writing residency just didn't make sense to most of the folks I know. Everyone from dear friends to colleagues wished me a great vacation. At least three wanted to come visit me during my "month off," dovetailing their vacation with mine. While I understood that my intention to write at least eight hours a day without having to think about anything or anyone from my "real life"—and without earning a cent in the process—was beyond their frame of reference, the misunderstanding still challenged me.

"This is not a vacation," I'd try to explain. "It is a chance to do personal work that means far more than any financial reward could ever offer."

"What do you owe the Soapstone people in exchange for your month?" they'd ask.

"Nothing," I'd say. "I owe myself the opportunity to dedicate my time and effort to my own writing for a change."

This, too, drew a blank.

For the most part, the writing I do for love exists in the very small margin around the writing I do for money. Most of the people I know don't have two parallel careers: one that pays a living and another that makes living worthwhile. They can't imagine sacrificing a month of income to do something that has no probable financial return for either the participant or the funder. Work beyond the boundaries of commerce: I was starting to feel revolutionary.

For the first two weeks, I wrote twelve hours a day. I was so desperate not to lose a second of this precious time that I ultimately shattered the hourglass of my adrenals. On day fourteen, I hit a wall of exhaustion. I hated myself. I hated my computer. I hated every word I had ever written, every word of literature ever published. And I wanted desperately to go home to my normal frenzy of getting-things-done. But I had signed an agreement not to leave, and if I broke that agreement and left, the other resident would also have to leave. So for two days, I forced myself to sit and read. I didn't try to write, forced myself not to even think about writing. Panic subsided to pacing, and then I finally hit my stride.

My days at Soapstone settled into a rhythm of nothing and everything: hauling wood in a wheelbarrow, maintaining the wood-burning stove day and night for sustainable heat, cooking and eating, reading, writing, and sleeping. Outside, free of the daily press of deadlines and traffic, of to-do and to-call lists, I got quiet. I got drenched in winter rains, and I became green with breathed-in earth and trees.

Each day I walked along the lichen-laden path beside Soapstone Creek. Nestled deep in the moss along the path is a community of gorgeous stones engraved with women's names. A binder inside the house tells the stories of the women for whom these stones are dedicated. I was particularly moved by a group of women who call themselves "The Graces." Students of a writing workshop given by author Grace Paley called "Flight of the Mind," they'd contributed a stone in her honor. In their tribute, the women listed a litany of the insight, wisdom, and spunk their instructor had communicated in only one week of teaching. My favorite was a recap of an interview in which Grace Paley was asked, "You're a mother, a wife, a writer, a teacher, an activist. How do you have time to do it all?" Grace responded, "Well, I have all day."

This little snippet of dialogue has come to represent what an entire month's worth of silence and solitude taught me. At Soapstone, I retrained myself to the truth that spaciousness is a choice. It was up to me to determine how expansive I would be with twenty-six consecutive "all days" belonging solely to me. The experience made me question: What am I so busy doing all day in my "real" life that I don't (or think I don't) have time to read, or talk to my neighbors, or pet my cat when he makes a spontaneous appearance in my lap, or to walk in the woods, or to read, think, feel, write? It was difficult to remember what was so damn much more important than being present in my life. I understood for the first time that I have all day every day, if that is how I choose to live it.

My bed at Soapstone was in a loft over the kitchen, accessible only by ladder. A long row of low windows on the south wall ran along the entire length of the bed, such that when I looked out through the rain-slicked glass, it seemed I was levitating over the trees.

Sleeping and daydreaming beside the raging creek, the container of self I'd arrived within was shaken loose, broken open.

I had come to Soapstone hoping to find my writing self—to claim and inhabit this archetype that had always seemed beyond my reach. One night as I listened to the creek shuddering downstream and allowed my mind to quiet, something clicked. One slow gear of truth turned and caught the next; the engine of my self-image was ignited into motion. I understood in that moment that I didn't need to leave my life to become a writer, that I'd been a writer my entire life.

In my mother's attic are boxes and boxes of notebooks filled with writing and writing practice, which I've kept since childhood, when I first began to write. For most of my adult life, I've made my living as a writer, and sometimes I'm paid as well or better than lawyers and doctors for what I do. I've been awarded scholarships and prizes for my writing. I've been published widely, and I am a monthly columnist for one journal and an assistant editor of another.

I lacked neither credentials nor external validation. What I lacked was belief in myself—until I lay hovering above Soapstone Creek, rushing ever forward beneath me. In that moment, I suddenly understood that the barrier blocking my access to the mystical World of Writers for thirty-five years was my mistaken notion that I didn't belong there, that I wasn't good enough. On that rain-illumined night, I gave the myth of Not Good Enough to the river, sent it off to dissipate in the ocean. During that fertile month at Soapstone, I learned that what I had long been seeking has always been available to me. Being a writer, the writer I'd longed to be, was simply a choice. One I was now ready to make.

~Sage Cohen

The Big Hiatus

A friend who also happens to be a writer recently mentioned he was taking a hiatus from writing for a week. The very idea floored me. Not write? For a whole week? Not anything? For me, that would be like taking a hiatus from breathing for a week.

Not that I'm one of those hyper-prolific writers we all love to hate. You know the people I'm talking about. The ones who get up at three in the morning and dash off a novel before lunchtime without having the decency to contract carpal tunnel syndrome. The ones who churn out more short stories in a month than most of us can hope to complete in a lifetime. The nerve of some people.

No, I'm not one of those. For me, a good paragraph may be all I can manage on a particular day. Oh, sure. Some days I churn out several pages, but most days I take what I can get, which is usually a few paragraphs. Don't get me wrong. I'm not slacking off. I work at my writing. It's just that if I try to function at a faster pace, what I end up with looks like someone fed a dictionary through a shredder. I have to give each piece however much time it requires of me. Otherwise, the results are stress and gibberish.

Nor am I one of those super-organized, highly efficient types. You've probably read countless articles on writing by these characters. Their day planners tend to look something like this:

5:00 A.M. to 5:02 A.M.—Fire up the computer and assemble writing materials

5:02 A.M. to 8:00 A.M.—Write fresh copy

8:02 A.M. to 8:07 A.M.—Stretch (optional bathroom break)

8:07 A.M. to 8:22 A.M.—E-mail submissions

8:22 A.M. to 8:37 A.M.—Phone calls

8:37 A.M. to 8:52 A.M.—Filing

8:52 A.M. to 9:54 A.M.—Revise fresh copy

9:54 A.M. to 9:59 A.M.—Stretch (and you really should take that bathroom break now)

And so on. You get the idea.

My day planner, on the other hand, looks more like a slightly soggy coaster. I write pretty much what I want, when I want. Filing doesn't even make the mental to-do list until the stacks of stacks cascade into each other, avalanche off the desk, and bury the cat. And as for firing up the computer, much of my writing isn't even done at the computer. I lie out on my swing and scrawl in a notebook, or sit in my armchair with my feet propped up and work on a clipboard, or sprawl on my office floor surrounded by index cards. Changing scenery and position helps keep me from feeling caged in.

I'm also not one of those savvy writers who stick to a niche, providing convenient marketing hooks for agents, publishers, and booksellers. These clever folks maximize efficiency and sales by writing the same types of things year in and year out. And many of them get really good at it.

Not me. I'm all over the map. I've written young reader books, short stories, poems, picture books, articles, adventures, mysteries, fantasies. You name it, I've tried it. Some of my books and stories have even been published. But let's face it. I've got the writer's version of ADHD. Oh, look! Here's an essay!

Yet, if nothing else, I am relentless. In spite of what some might call a haphazard approach to writing, not a day goes by that I don't get something written. All the surfaces in my office are littered with projects in various stages of completion. My computer is packed with manuscripts. My shelves groan under filled notebooks and scraps of paper covered in ideas and dialogue and interesting turns of phrase.

When I shower, I scheme of new torments to heap on my characters. When I wait in line at the store, I study mannerisms to give to my fictional people. When I exercise, I talk out plot problems with my husband. When I go on vacation, some of the first things I pack are pens and paper, so I can make notes on scene descriptions and interesting characters I meet. When I go to a restaurant, I memorize funny comments I overhear for later transcription. When I go to bed at night, I keep pen and paper in my nightstand for those times I wake up with an idea so brilliant I absolutely must scribble it down so I won't forget it. Though, to be honest, most of the scribbles I make in the middle of the night turn out, in the light of day, to be either illegible or cryptic beyond comprehension. Still, I forge ahead.

Some people may call me crazy. You can call me what you like. Just as long as you call me a writer.

I tried to imagine this so-called hiatus, this week without writing. What would I do with all those quirky thoughts that constantly pop into my head? Ignore them? Push them away? Let them die, never to have their shot at entertaining strangers I'll never meet? And what about all those experiences? The neighbor kids pulling up all the survey flags from the new development site to play with them? The geese and goslings swimming across the pond? The friend with the secret crush? The smell of fresh cucumbers from the garden? I couldn't just leave it all unwritten, could I?

No, I couldn't.

So I told my friend all this. I asked him to explain this wacky concept of his, this "hiatus from writing." And do you know what he said? He confessed that he is just as incapable of taking time off from writing as I am, that he was only taking a hiatus from a particular project. When it came to writing, he said, "I am married to it. Everything in life is centered around it."

"Oh, okay," I told him, my feathers unruffling as my world fell back into place. "That sounds more like it."

~Denise R. Graham

Out of the Fog

W here do you get your ideas?"

Does the girl in the back row really want to know, or did her teacher assign a certain number of questions that students must ask me, the visiting writer? The teacher looks at me. Hope shines from her eyes. Will I enlighten her students by giving them The Right Answer—that I dutifully sit at my desk for an hour and free-write onto a yellow legal pad until I perfect my ideas, which I then neatly organize into appropriate file folders? Most teachers love the idea of free-writing and organization. They hate that I tell their students free-writing is a waste of time and that I'm disorganized.

I want to tell the class that I don't get ideas. Ideas get me. Instead, I describe how I write.

"I compose directly onto my computer," I tell them. "Of my three computers, the eMac is my favorite.

I like its sleek whiteness—like an empty page waiting to be filled. The white keys require so little pressure, the delete key removes evidence of my mistakes, and the 17-inch screen is easy to see through my bifocals."

The students laugh. Bifocals aren't yet part of their reality.

"My eMac, solid and substantial, sits on my cluttered desk in my equally cluttered study."

The teacher smiles at my alliteration. "Solid and substantial" sounds so writerish.

"Some writers work best in an environment devoid of clutter and animals; I am not one of those writers. Cats nap on my cluttered desk." Digressing, I tell them about my six cats.

The students nod. Teenagers are not strangers to clutter or pets.

"Some say that a cluttered desk is the sign of a cluttered mind." I glance at the teacher's desk. The few papers on it are neatly stacked. "One thing a writer needs is a cluttered mind—one so brimming over with ideas that she has plenty to pick and choose from."

The teacher cringes, but I continue. "I never wonder what I can write about. Instead, I wonder what idea I will work on next. An idea always claws its way to the top of the heap that is both my desktop and my imagination. If that idea doesn't grab me, another lurks beneath it."

A few students lean forward. Maybe I'm saying something worth listening to. At least I'm not telling them to free-write. And I use technology—three computers!

"From my study window, I can see the Blue Ridge Mountains in the distance. They're beyond the hill, beyond the trees, beyond the cornfield across the road. The view from my study window reflects what a writer ought to have: a series of beyonds. Just beyond one idea is another."

A few students look out the classroom window. They see the houses across the street.

"A writer should be able to see into the distance," I tell them. "Or at least know what is out there. On a clear day, I can see the Peaks of Otter. On a foggy day, I still know they're there. The same with ideas— somewhere in the fog and the clutter, ideas are out there."

I figure I should tell how I structure my stories. Teachers like that.

"Usually I write the ending to a story first. I like to see where I'm going. Writer Lee Smith says that she writes her last line first and tapes it up where she can see it. I type mine so I can see it. Whenever I open a blank document, I stare at the shiny white page on the shiny white eMac's screen: all that empty white space—like fog."

The students nod. Some haven't the foggiest idea who Lee Smith is.

"Then I type my last line. My words shimmer on the screen. The fog lifts. I can see where I'm going. Some writers carefully plot their stories and structure every minute detail. They're probably the ones who, before they take a trip, peruse the road map and carefully plot their route along the fastest and shortest route to their destination—usually the Interstate.

"I don't do that. I like to explore the back roads and admire the scenery. As long as I know my destination, I don't mind an occasional wrong turn. I can always turn around."

Great! the teacher probably thinks. *This writer hasn't the foggiest idea what she's talking about.*

I plunge ahead. "Some writers might say, 'Oh, but I want my story to reflect life! In life, we don't know where we're going to end!' But we do know exactly where we'll end."

I pause for dramatic effect. Let it sink in that I'm talking about death.

"Everyone has the same ending. The only difference is how we get there. I know my destination, and I want to get there in the most interesting way."

A few nod their agreement. I tell them how I don't do all of my writing in my study—how most of my writing takes place in my head while I'm doing something else. I tell them I've heard a couple of speakers at writing conferences say that a writer should sit down at the computer every day and wait for an idea to come. "'Put your butt in the chair!' I heard one spokeswoman at a conference declare."

The kids giggle. I said the word "butt" out loud, right in the classroom.

"My best ideas come while I'm doing something else," I tell them, "so I haul my derriere out of the chair and do something else—laundry, vacuuming, playing with the cats, or walking with my dogs—until I get an idea. Sometimes I take my iBook a couple of miles down the road to my farm. While my dogs run through the woods, I perch on the tailgate of my old Dodge truck and write. A writer can go where the action is. Sometimes a writer can even join the action—or doggedly follow a trail of thought or bat ideas around like a playful cat."

Did the teacher notice my simile?

"Once in a while, I use my old iMac in the den. While I work at the iMac, Buford the deaf cat sleeps on top of the computer armoire. He doesn't like anything to creep up on him, so he sleeps high. Dylan, my smallest black cat, drapes himself over the iMac. He puts his front leg through the handle so he doesn't slide off. Sometimes I have to move his tail so I can see what I've written. Cats are a great audience. They never find fault with anything I write."

The students laugh. The teacher smiles a little.

"At the iMac, I can look sideways out the back door to the pasture and watch my horses graze. My view is limited—a line of trees, the edge of the barn, and two elderly mares."

Most of the students—even a few on the back row—are listening now.

"Sometimes a writer needs a limited view, a narrow focus. Sometimes a sidewise glance is what I need to get a fresh idea. Sometimes, like Dylan, I hang on to an idea so I don't slip away from it. Sometimes, like Buford, I don't let outside ideas creep up on me. Sometimes, like my mares, my imagination grazes."

I want to tell them how my horses will unroll a round bale of hay. They'll paw and push at it until it yields to their efforts and unrolls all over the pasture. Then they'll eat the good stuff from the middle. I want to use the unrolling of the hay as a metaphor for unrolling an idea—how the good stuff is in the middle and how you can't see it from the outside—but time is running out. Several students glance at the clock. I do too.

I wrap it up: "Each computer gives me a different viewpoint, a different approach. A writer, I've decided, can't have too many computers—or too many viewpoints."

Yeah, yeah, the kids think. *Hurry up, so we can go.*

I speak faster. "Years ago, I believed that ideas had to flow from my brain, down my arm, into my fingertips, and out my pen onto a yellow legal pad. Then, after much crossing out and revising, I'd bang away on my typewriter until the idea popped out onto paper. What a waste of time! Now, ideas—like electric currents—flow from brain to fingertips to screen. I can move words, sentences, paragraphs; I can insert and delete. Quick as a cat, I can change the whole look of my manuscript in seconds. I can luxuriate in words that appear before my eyes almost as fast as they appear in my mind."

I look at the teacher. She nods slightly and points to the clock.

"Where do I get my ideas?" Seconds before the bell rings, I give my answer: "All sorts of places."

~Becky Mushko

The Echolalia of Literature

D on't wake me up; I don't like it!" I shouted, as David, our autistic son, burst into our bedroom, talking loudly to himself about which pants to wear to work. He had placed his shoes in his father's closet when they were still new—donated them—so that he could keep wearing his old, familiar shoes. Now he had apparently decided the new shoes had been around long enough to wear, but storing them in our closet had become part of his routine.

That evening, as I worked on a series of poems I was writing about David, I heard him walking from room to room, repeating, "Don't woke me up; I don't like it." He echoed the words I had said to him that morning, but changed my verb to past tense to reflect the time change. Echolalia, the repetition of words spoken by another person, is common in people with autism. Sometimes, as here, the words are delayed, coming hours, days, or even years after the person has heard them.

At twenty-five, David—a tall, thin man who appeared normal except for exaggerated body movements and extreme self-absorption—lived with my husband and me and his younger brother and sister. In spite of his limited ability to communicate, his almost continuous self-talk (similar to a tape of his thoughts) provided a needed window into his thinking.

Writing about David in journal entries and poems for the past two years, I had begun to feel a strange blending of his consciousness with my own. One reason for this was that I could not avoid comparing his thought processes to mine. Besides, as in the previous example, he often repeated my words as he walked around the house. A further reason may have been his habit—characteristic of those with autism—of exchanging the pronouns "I" and "you."

The following journal entry depicts the melding that can occur because of his pronoun confusion:

Today David accidentally bumped into me as we put groceries away in the kitchen. "I'm in my way," he said, bending over to press the place on my leg his foot had touched—a gesture I've often seen him make, as if he is trying to restore something that has been altered. Since it is common for him to use "I" and "you" and

*"my" and "your" interchangeably, it was unclear who
he thought was in the other's way. But I was reminded
of the expression, "I get in my own way."*

As I wrote about David (or so I thought), I kept
seeing my own struggle to make sense of the world
mirrored in his. In one poem, "April Walk with
David," I wrote of being lost together as we walked
the trails at Sunriver, Oregon, while his father and
siblings bicycled on the same trails:

*We walk the same circuitous paths
        his brother and sister ride
through bitterbrush and pine.*

*When his long legs take him too
        far ahead, I shout Wait!
Cyclists sing out from behind*

*Passing on the left, and I pull him
        right. Once I got us
lost. Even blue and orange*

*arrows on the asphalt and a color-
        coded map could not
bring us home. Yield . . . Yield.*

He pauses before the yellow sign
    at one intersection, runs
his fingers over the letters. Stop? . . . .

In another poem, "The Wishful Undoing," I expressed David's reaction when two large split-trunk maples plummeted in our backyard during an ice storm. "We'll stop the wind. / The trees won't fall down, they won't," he'd said as we huddled by the fire. Later, while two men cut the trees with chainsaws, he pleaded from the window, "They won't cut the trees, they won't." Whenever possible, I use his own words in an attempt to convey his voice.

I think I had several reasons for writing these poems about my son: to exorcise my own grief over his autism, to explore his thoughts and feelings for myself and for the reader, and to show that his thoughts and feelings are not much different from anyone else's.

Writing about a family member is never easy. One worries about overstepping the bounds of family loyalty. It's particularly daunting when the person written about cannot communicate well. I wondered, *Was I presenting David fairly? If he understood what I was doing, would he consent to it?* I think he had some idea that I was writing about him. Sometimes he stood near my desk and watched me as I wrote, but never questioned what I was doing. Once he seemed to spot his name and posted the poem about himself on the refrigerator, where he kept his performance awards from work. I will have to take this as his blessing.

Some journal entries did not make their way into poems. They remain in my journal, and I hope some-day to weave them into a book. The poems, begun ten years ago now, have not been published as a series, though I have submitted them to many chapbook contests. It would be easy to doubt their value.

We belong to a culture that expects things to happen rapidly and believes it best to replace the old with the new. On the hill where I live near Portland, Oregon, one-acre lots are being turned into several small lots. A bulldozer razes a quirky old house or a stately one to make way for six or seven of the latest McMansions.

This practice conflicts with the wisdom that important things take time to develop and with the truth that objects do not lose value simply because they are old. How large a leap would it be from con-sidering old houses as dispensable to viewing people who are old or disabled in the same way?

As writers, we can be a powerful force against the common thinking of our society. We speak with individual voices of things that are difficult, strange, uplifting, or simply worthy of attention. We can't stop because a piece doesn't get published or because no one seems to care that it's been written. Of course, this runs counter to ego and the sense that one must get on with his or her life.

One of the hardest things for me as a writer has been to allow enough time for the writing to develop. I once heard a produce expert explain how to pick a good watermelon: "If the ground spot—the part that's rested on the earth—is yellow to white, the melon is ripe. If that spot's light green, the melon's still green." This simple advice may also apply to a fiction or non-fiction piece or a poem. Since it too is alive and growing, it takes time to develop, time for the writer to determine its center. It was a surprise to me to learn that a piece of writing could change color simply because it had rested a few days (or weeks or years) on my desk or in a drawer. Of course, it wasn't the writing that had changed; I had.

Sometimes, when I'm discouraged about the slowness of my writing, I think of something David once said as he made a lunch for work the next day: "You make your own ham-cheese-pickle sandwich. You're doing pretty good!" We all need to celebrate our accomplishments—especially writers. In a sense, we're all making our own sandwiches—a few pickles at a time.

For the last five years, David has lived in a group home about twenty minutes from our house, and we see him on weekends and vacations. Because of medication he now takes, he is less anxious and his self-talk has decreased, making it more difficult to know what he is thinking.

Remembering David's interpretation of my words, "Don't wake me up; I don't like it," I think how parents' admonitions may echo for a day—or even years—in their children's heads. And how much parents learn from their children. I also think of the positive effect that writers have upon one another and upon their culture. One might call it the echolalia of literature, a continuous blending of ideas as they pass from one person to the next.

~Phyllis Ann Mannan

The author's poem "April Walk with David" was published in the *Oregonian* (2000).

Addiction

Like a junkie consumed by meth or crack, I've long battled with a drug I can't quit. I get itchy, nervous, and paranoid when I've gone too long without it. When I seek it out, I'm both scared to get it and scared not to. With it, I'm high as the Sears Tower—but one dose is never enough. I need to have a little every so often just to keep myself going. My husband knows I'm hopelessly hooked, so he leaves me alone as I pursue my addiction: publication.

Oh, I know plenty of writers are afflicted. I must be especially vulnerable to it, though, because I'm not even a professional freelance writer. I can't make it my job, because what if I couldn't get enough of the goods to keep myself going? After all, when publication is your drug, you need more than just cash and a dealer. You need to prove your talent to the right person at the right time, and your writing must possess some mysterious "it" factor that only editors can detect. It's exhausting. I refuse to put that joy-killing pressure on myself, to depend on it for my subsistence. So I tell myself I'll have just a little, and that'll be enough. Of course, it never is.

Like all addicts, I make excuses. I blame it on other people. My friends and family—and the book-store clerk and the gas-station attendant and the postman—all expect a byline, and I must deliver! Actually, though, I'm my own worst enemy. A survivor of a brutally impressive academic career, I realize I'm supposed to Do Something With My Life. Expectation smothers me like a down parka in summertime. I cope by wallowing in my drug-related behavior: I write all the time. I write during my Friday-morning personal time, at my day job assisting an attorney, through enraged letters to the editor and e-mails to friends and letters to grandparents. I even write to myself, making lists and logs and notes and memos. Nothing is too insignificant to put on paper. I keep a pen with me at all times to avoid panic attacks. But it's under control. Really.

I'll never forget my first major high, many years past, an event that would secure my fate as a life-long junkie. I had read and enjoyed *Chocolate for a Woman's Heart*, a short-story anthology. When I saw that the editor was accepting submissions for a series of similar books, I took a chance, writing and submitting a story. Shortly thereafter, I came home to find a message on my answering machine from the editor herself. She had called to tell me how much she enjoyed the story and to say she might put it in a future book.

I remember being stunned, thrilled—hooked—and yet she hadn't even slipped me the hard stuff. That was to come a few months later, when she told me she wanted to see more of my writing. I quickly set to work on three new stories, praying one would catch her eye, and sent them in. Her next call to me was like a needle to the vein: "You hit the jackpot," she said, a smile in her voice. "I'm going to publish all three." After I got off the phone, I became a whirlwind of screaming, jumping, flailing excitement, similar to the time my unrequited college crush suddenly asked me out.

That's how they hook you, though; you get some product, and it tastes so sweet you know you'll do anything to get more. The problem is, it's rarely easy to get your fix. Most of the time, I'm down, anxious, deflated. On bad days, I try to remember there's more to writing than publication.

Seeking encouragement recently, I looked up "writer" in the dictionary. Unfortunately, Webster's primary definitions imply, you know, actually publishing stuff, but I kept reading and was pacified, temporarily, by the third definition: "a person who commits his or her thoughts, ideas, etc., to writing" and the fifth: "a person who writes or is able to write." So, yes, I get points for committing to my craft, and yes, I am a real writer—but Webster's reassurances couldn't console me when my first literary magazine rejection arrived in the mail. It was a typed form letter, of course, with a "handwritten" note of generic encouragement at the bottom that appeared suspiciously photocopied. My suspicions were confirmed with rejection letter number two, identical to the first. Clearly, this editor didn't want to be my dealer, but that didn't stop him from asking me for money anyway: Would I like to subscribe? In my weakened state, I considered it.

Temporary relief from my addiction arrived when my writing friend, Melanie, sent me the first few chapters of her book for review and editing. She and I met online after scoring the same fix—publication in the same anthology—and friendship developed. I dove into Melanie's book eagerly, happy to be doing something productive with my time that didn't bring a cloud of publication anxiety with it. I redlined. I corrected grammar, made conceptual suggestions, and raised new questions. I marked up the manuscript and composed a separate document, breaking down my thoughts and giving feedback page by page. It was the most fun I'd had in months, working with words and yet freed of worries about whether an editor was going to want to publish me—because it wasn't about me. It was about Melanie. I bundled up the manuscript and my comments and mailed them to her.

A couple of weeks later, a package arrived in the mail, a small brown box labeled with Melanie's return address. In it, I found a thank-you note and a pair of earrings: white, sparkling stones set in a flower pattern. I was surprised, moved, and delighted. The earrings were, and are, beautiful. Regardless of their retail value, I consider them priceless. They're worth even more than publication.

The earrings took on a special meaning for me, changing the way I view my addiction. They helped me see that publication isn't truly the drug I crave. Publication is just a small part of something bigger— validation. It's that feeling of, yes, I accomplished something of value. It's thank-you earrings from Melanie. It's being treated to dinner by a grateful friend because I rewrote her business's advertising. It's the dedication of my husband's master's thesis, made to me because I have inspired him with my "attention to detail and tremendous ability to focus on a task," the skills I use when I pursue my writing goals.

Now, I would never claim I don't need publication.

I still want that fix, and I still stumble around seeking it, desperate and determined. With my new insight, though, I realize that when no dealer will deal to me, I have other options. I don't have to be published to know that my work is worthwhile. Validation is far more obtainable than publication, and it comes from everywhere: from friends, from family, from the people I help with the skills that I have. Maybe someday I'll even find it within myself. Until then, I'll just put on my sparkly flower earrings, pick up my pen, and keep writing.

~Alaina Smith

Heritage of Words

All elementary schools smell the same, I thought, as we walked into Ben's school for our first parent-teacher conference of first grade: drying paint, chalk, and freshly sharpened pencils.

Ben jumped and pointed at everything he saw all the way down the hall to his classroom. "Look, those are pictures the teachers drew," he said, pointing. "Hi, Mr. Oberg!" he called, waving and high-fiving his principal as they passed each other. Mr. Oberg grinned and returned the greeting. "My classroom's over here," he directed us.

"We know, Ben," I said. But he was in his element, and he wanted to be in charge of leading us to his classroom.

I watched my son in amazement. *He's so much like his dad,* I thought, *a carbon copy of my social, energetic, intelligent husband.* Both were boys all the way through—knights in search of a cause to fight for and a damsel to defend. Ben was born giving orders and leading people; I knew he was destined for great things.

Truth be told, I found it hard to relate to my oldest son. His energy, his outgoing nature, his overwhelming "boyness"—I just couldn't find much common ground with him. When I was a child, I was shy and serious, not outgoing and fun. I wanted to be a good mother to this child, wanted to encourage him in his pursuits, but it seemed so hard to find a way to do that when I couldn't connect with him.

Ben's teacher, Mrs. Castellanos, welcomed us into her tidy and organized classroom and beckoned us to sit down. "Ben, do you want to listen to a book on tape while I talk to Mom and Dad?" she offered. Ben nodded, selected a tape and tape recorder, and found a quiet spot to listen to the book.

Mrs. Castellanos—"Mrs. C.," as the students called her—pulled out Ben's progress report. "Here's where we are for the first term," she said.

I had to admit, I was pleasantly surprised: almost all plusses or check plusses, indicating he was mostly right on track.

"He's a bright boy," Mrs. Castellanos told us. "He gets a little hyper sometimes, but usually I just tell him to sit back down, and he does. He's a good kid."

Mrs. Castellanos pulled out a book of lined paper

stapled together and labeled First Grade Journal, October, 2005. "I wanted to show you Ben's story," she said. "I give the kids a few minutes every day to write in their journals, and Ben has been pulling together a story."

A story? As we leaned over to read the hesitant first-grade handwriting, my heart skipped a beat. There it was—a story, with a beginning, middle, and end, paragraphs, punctuation, a plot, dialogue, even multiple characters. A good guy, a bad guy, an adventure. Kings and queens with swords, no doubt inspired by a recent reading of *The Lion, the Witch, and the Wardrobe*. A wolf, a journey . . . all from Ben's imagination.

"He did this over several days," Mrs. Castellanos explained. "This is really advanced for a first grader. He kept the plot going for the most part, and he remembered each day where he'd left off and where to go next. I knew you'd want to read it."

I stared at my little guy, listening to his book at the other side of the room—the child I couldn't relate to, didn't "get" much of the time. He was a boy—loud, boisterous, and physical–and I was used to girls. I was a girl raised in a family of girls, and when I'd found out I was having a boy, I'd nearly cried. "I don't know what to do with boys!" I lamented to my husband. He assured me I'd learn what to do with our little miracle, our child conceived after two years of trying, but I found only limited comfort in his words. I worried, *How on earth would I relate to this boy?*

Ben was social from day one; he smiled at everyone and was happiest in a big circle of people. With my reserved nature, I was happiest with one or two really good friends. Again I worried, *How could I ever relate to my little social butterfly?*

As he grew, Ben exhibited a strong will that stretched the limits of my patience. If I had a button that could be pushed, Ben would find it and push it. If we said, "Don't go over that line," he would walk on the line. I did not understand that willful nature. I worried, *How can I manage a child who won't stay within the boundaries I set for him?* As a mother, I wanted to have some common ground with each of my children, and it had been easy for me to find it with the three children who followed Ben. Chloe, my first daughter, was a girly girl, quiet and serious, who loved mothering her dolls and could easily sleep a whole morning away—just like Mom. Sam was a musician, and he had a bevy of allergies that required constant vigilance—just like Mom. Natalie was shy, reserved, and often overwhelmed by large groups and loud noises—just like Mom. But how could I relate to Ben?

And there it was: Ben was a writer. I am a writer. My son is a writer. All the stories in his head, all the imaginary friends, all the dramatic energy, all the early language skills—it all now made sense. Ben was a writer—just like Mom. And with one teacher's thoughtful gesture, I found common ground with my son.

Being a writer isn't something that just happens when a child learns to write letters and put them together into words and sentences. It's something you're born with, discover, and develop. It's something that makes us writers "weird" to other people. When people ask how I got into writing, I always have to say, honestly, that I've always been a writer. I've always walked around with characters, dialogue, and stories in my head, and I didn't realize until my early twenties that most people don't. I once asked my husband what he had in his head, if not stories, and he gave me a slightly bemused, furrowed expression. "Other stuff," he said.

I'm sure I confused my own mother with my writing. She used to give me that same slightly bemused expression when I would launch into some imaginative tale constructed in my own head. She never criticized or discouraged me; in fact, quite the opposite, she always encouraged my love of language and stories. But she has confessed to me that my penchant for putting words together into stories doesn't come from her. "It's your dad," she told me once.

"Sometimes I'm with him and I realize he's in another place. I don't know where his head goes, but I think he's just creating. His mom is that way, too. They're just wired to create stories."

I do remember occasionally stumbling across some notebook of my father's with a few lines of prose or poetry scrawled across in that peculiarly neat handwriting of someone trained by the U.S. Air Force and the local police bureau. I sometimes asked him what he was writing, but he never really gave any distinct answers. He'd usually just shrug it off and change the subject. His work, like that of many other writers, was intensely personal.

A certain loneliness comes with being in the community of writers. Most of my family and friends are not part of that community, and as much as they love and support me, they can't go to the same places I go in my own mind. They just don't have the writer's wiring.

Watching my son listen to a book, I know that in his head, the story has taken on a life of its own. Where the tape leaves off, he'll continue the story and create new adventures and characters in his head. He'll probably act them out with his brother and sisters. He may even write a few down in his journal. I can say this with certainty, because it's how I'm wired, too. At last, we have a way to relate.

I know I can encourage Ben in this. I want him—all of my children—to have the freedom and support to pursue their creative passions. While I may not always understand the creative passions of my other children, I'll understand Ben on a deep level that only another writer can recognize. He'll never look at me when he's weaving a story and see a puzzled furrow on my forehead. Instead, I'll likely ask him, "What happens next?"

Ben and I share this: a heritage of words. A literary legacy that stretches back to my father and his mother before him . . . back farther still to the beginning of humankind, when the first storyteller wove the first tale to pass on to his heirs. It's a noble heritage. I know my son will do it justice.

~Amy Rose Davis

Nonfiction Nightmares

I wish I were a fiction writer. I would give my characters their sorrows but also neatly wrapped, maybe even sappy-happy, endings—the kind that don't seem to happen in my life. I'm usually left wondering what happened and then spend years trying to figure it out, which is one of the reasons I write nonfiction. By writing my life, my truth, I make sense of the world around me. I also feel as though my writing connects me to other people, because I know I'm not the only one wandering confused through life. I hope my stories make them feel a little better.

Therein lies a problem: Although I write nonfiction (memoir), it often reads like fiction. I write with the maxim "show don't tell" firmly planted in my mind, leading people to believe I am writing fiction. "We would be proud to publish your short story," read one letter. I wrote back, "Thank you, and it is nonfiction, as stated in my cover letter."

In one nonfiction piece, I did a little memoiristic "telling," submitted it, and received a personalized rejection letter calling it a "personal essay." While I was pleased that the editor thought my piece had enough merit to write me an actual letter, I wanted to write back and say, "I know what a personal essay is, and this isn't one. I'm just telling a story. It's a true story, but is there no room in the world for nonfiction that 'shows' like fiction?" When my nonfiction feels like fiction, people want me to tidy things up to make it "read better." The structure of a recent piece is my telephone calls to my ex-lover, who, in the course of our four-year relationship, almost never came to my house and hardly ever called me. But the piece started:

The phone rings.

"Hello?" my lover acts as if I had been the one to call him. He is late, and I ask him when he'll be over.

Two, count 'em, two problems in the first three lines. Writer friends said, "But he never calls you," and "I thought you always went to his house." I didn't think it necessary to start the piece with an explanation about how, in the last few months of our relationship, he'd acquired a roommate and started coming to my apartment so we could have some privacy. Or how he did call me a few times over the years. Besides, it is made clear in the next three lines why he is calling me:

"There's a problem . . ." he says. He's stingy with his words. To make up for the lack of them, he draws them out. ". . . I, uhhhhh, kind of got together with this woman last night at sweat lodge."

But the one phone call he initiates in the fifteen pages of the "story" still bothers people who've read my previous memoir pieces, because calling me is out of character for him.

Then there's a third problem: sweat lodge. My writers' group assumed he was Native American. He's not. But by the time the physical description comes, some of them wanted him to be an Indian and were disgruntled to discover he was white. One person, still unclear of his race after reading the description, actually suggested I make him white—as if he were a fictional character whose ethnicity is within my control.

So here's how the story starts now:

*The phone rings. It's my lover. He rarely calls me, so
I ask if he's okay.*

*"There's a problem." He's stingy with his words.
"I kind of got together with this woman last night."*

But my trials weren't over. The next suggestion was
that I cut my next love interest (who was African American) completely. And my group didn't want my ex's current lover to be Asian and from Hong Kong. I expected
the next comment to be that I should transform myself
into Minnesota Lutheran instead of California Jew.

Had I been a fiction writer, I could have avoided
this predicament entirely. My ex could have been a
white man who met a white woman at the Lutheran
Church in the small Minnesota town in which we all
lived. It would have been a lot neater that way.

But I'm writing nonfiction and feel compelled to
stick as closely to the truth as possible. After all, this
business of truth-telling is sometimes painful. The
wrecked bits of my life that I have shoved under the
bed to mingle with the dust monsters in dark places
eventually have to be swept out into the light—to be
either vacuumed up and banished forever, or dusted
off and examined. That is when I sit down to write.
When I'm finished, the question foremost in my mind
is, Did the truth make a good story?

But these days, when the line between fiction and nonfiction is blurring, distinguishing the truth from lies seems a little difficult . . . as my Intro to Creative Writing students discovered.

"What's the difference between fiction and non-fiction?" I asked.

All twenty of them agreed that fiction is made up and nonfiction is true. They were disabused of that notion by a memoirist who spoke to our class. He had written a scene in which he bribes his New York landlord. The landlord has a slavering dog straining at the leash, so the writer gives the dog a payoff as well. After reading this section of his memoir, he told students that the scene was the "literary truth" rather than the "literal truth." The writer wanted his readers to feel his precarious mental state—recently sober Minnesota boy, new to the big bad city of New York. He did pay off the landlord, but the dog belonged to someone else and he was never afraid of it. Furthermore, he couldn't remember the furniture in that particular apartment, so he made it up.

In our next class some of my students said they felt betrayed by the writer. Yes, betrayed. They were expecting the literal truth.

They asked, "Can he do that and still call it nonfiction?"

"Yes, he can," I said.

"Would you make things up?"

I said, "No, I wouldn't. I will not make up dialogue or attribute it to somebody who didn't say it. I will not give a pet-less person a dog. I will not invent furniture. But you need to decide for yourselves what you consider the truth."

We spent the next month debating the literal versus the literary (or emotional) truth of a situation. By the end of the semester the class was still divided. One group felt inventing details was fine as long as it served the emotional truth of the story; the other group thought if writers had to invent details, then they should call it autobiographical fiction.

I, of course, fall into that second group. Yes, I realize what I write is my truth, what I experienced. Doubtless, others do not experience the same situation in the same way—for example, my mother. I love her, but we do not inhabit the same reality.

Here's a typical encounter with Mom:

On my last visit to my parent's house in Arizona, my family told me we were having high tea at the Phoenician, a five-star hotel.

"What time are we leaving for tea, Mom?" I asked.

"Three o'clock." She disappeared into her walk-in closet—twice as big as my apartment bathroom—and came back out dropping a pair of open-toed shoes on the floor. "Try these," she said.

"Mom, you wear a size five; I wear a seven."

"Just try them."

I am nearly forty years old. I have been wearing a size seven for twenty-five years, yet nearly every time I visit, she tries to get me to wear her shoes.

"They won't fit."

"What shoes are you wearing?" She asked.

"My black boots."

"Those old combat boots? You can't wear those."

"They're all I brought with me." I told her if I had known we were going somewhere fancy, I would have brought the proper attire.

"What pants are you wearing?"

"My jeans," I said.

"You can't wear jeans! Try some of my pants," she urged.

I said, "I'm not wearing your pants. You are five feet tall and a size twelve. I am five foot seven and a size eight." I didn't remind her that she wears only capris, which would float somewhere around my knees.

I will say two things about the above conversation. First, there is no doubt in my mind that my mother felt she was being rational. It wouldn't matter if everyone read this essay and agreed (with me) that she was being irrational, she would trot out fifty different reasons why what she said made perfect sense.

Second, it is recollected, not precisely recorded, dialogue, but my mother's words have a tendency to burn themselves into my brain—as do images. Even before I started writing seriously, all those sentences that used to float through my head were lines that belonged in my stories. Pictures spooling through my mind—the flatbed truck, piled three-high with bales of hay, a coyote-like dog pacing on top as the vehicle sped along at seventy-five miles an hour just outside of Modesto—belonged in my writing. Observations about people—the way my ex-lover jerked his jaw to one side, to get the words out—belonged on the page.

But the more my nonfiction stories appear in print, the more I wonder how the people I write about feel when they read themselves on the page. So far nobody I know—not even my ex-lover—has objected to anything, but there's the key word—know. I've known some strange people. People who, say, might come after me with a kitchen knife—or a lawyer—if they don't like what I have to say. So mostly, I don't write about them. On the rare occasion I do, I won't change dialogue or make up something that didn't happen, but I will change names and identifying characteristics.

On the other hand, as a wise woman recently asked, "What are the chances that person will even read it?" Then I knew the concern wasn't so much about the strange characters I've known than it was about my mother. What if what I wrote made her feel bad—or cry? And what would she think of me?

After I was finished feeling stupid—nearly forty and still anxious about disappointing or upsetting my mother—I consoled myself with the thought that I am not alone. Most of my nonfiction-writing friends worry and wonder what impact exposing details about themselves and their families will have—especially on their mothers. Granted, I don't have to show my story to her. But now that it's been published, I picture her finding a copy lying around my apartment on one of her visits to Minneapolis—she likes to clean my apartment when I'm at school. I'd come home and find her sitting in the middle of my couch, face in her hands.

"What's wrong, Mom?" I'd say.

She'd look up, wave a copy of the magazine at me, and there would be tears. There would be guilt. She would wail, "Where did I go wrong? Wasn't I a good mother to you?"

No, it wouldn't happen like that. Despite our differences, my mother has always been my biggest supporter—in whatever I choose to pursue. This is what would happen: She would lay the magazine carefully on the table and say, "I'm proud of you. I'm glad your writing is going so well, but once your book is published, I think you should tell me which chapters I might want to skip. There are some things a mother doesn't want to know." And she would smile.

But still, I worry. Now, if I were a fiction writer, I wouldn't lose sleep about ambiguous endings, who said what, defamation of character, or what my mother might think. I could just make things up, and instead of that sad, or at best bittersweet ending, I'd give my character a happy ending. And I guess this is why I don't write fiction. Life isn't neat and tidy. Life doesn't get wrapped up in pretty paper with a bow: Here's your present. It's your happy life in a box. Instead, I like to quote my father, "You get what you get." And as I always add, sometimes it's enough.

~Ellen Dworsky

This story was first published in the literary journal *Rattle*, Winter 2002.

The Baptism

I can see her only dimly now, although I do remember mousy brown hair, and a slightly pockmarked complexion. The picture engraved in my memory is a profile view, taken from across the room. In my mind's eye, she is half-sitting, half-standing behind a tall desk, leaning forward, intent, straining with all her will to inculcate a love of the English language into the hearts of twenty-eight teenage girls whose thoughts right now, as always, are anywhere but on Miss H. and her lesson plan.

If my picture of Miss H. were in a frame, an inscription underneath it would read: "Here is a teacher who touched my soul."

Miss H. had never known, of course, that anything she'd said had such a profound effect on me. I did not realize it myself until half a century later.

I was a newcomer to her classroom, having been

demoted from another class for a combination of poor marks and bad behavior. Some of the staff were wary of me on that account, but not so Miss H. Her focus was not on reputation but on the work at hand.

If one can believe the nostalgic posts on the old school's Internet discussion board, Miss H. was a teacher to be feared, but I certainly do not remember her that way. I do recall that she seemed a very private person. Our geography teacher, Miss K., still wore her sapphire engagement ring as a token of fidelity to a soldier who would never return, and there were rumors that a similarly romantic story surrounded Miss H. In those immediate post-war days, it might well have been true. But we could never find out, no matter how boldly we displayed our curiosity. At a personal level, Miss H. remained an enigma.

She did have a passion, though, and one day, I discovered what it was. She adored poetry. And poetry, as it so happened, was to be our class topic for the next few weeks.

Always fond of writing and fascinated by words, I took to poetry like the proverbial duck. My classmates seemed bored by reading it and severely challenged when it came to writing their own, but I loved doing both. While they struggled and grumbled and chewed the ends of their pencils, I happily corralled my unruly thoughts into the strict enclosures of rhyme and meter.

When Miss H. considered us sufficiently educated in the traditional forms and everyone in class at least knew what iambic pentameter was, even if they could not use it very well, Miss H. announced it was time to introduce us to free verse. She would read us a poem by D. H. Lawrence. It was called "Snake." By the time she had read the first three lines, I was no longer sitting at that wooden desk in my school uniform. I was D. H. Lawrence, in his pajamas, in the middle of a hot and sultry afternoon, telling the story of the snake who came to drink at his water trough. I saw it all, heard it, smelled it, felt it. I was there.

Miss H. read beautifully. I knew, in that moment, that she was there too, in that hot courtyard, just as I was. No one else seemed particularly moved by the poem. It felt as though Miss H. and I had gone to a secret place together, leaving the rest of the class far behind. We had shared a few moments of special intimacy, just the two of us. Even now, fifty-four years later, whenever I think of that poem or reread it, my insides turn a little somersault. It is not exactly pleasure. It is perhaps best described as a gut-level recognition of the power of words to evoke atmosphere, to hint at deeper layers of meaning, to stir up thought and feeling, to inspire.

Our homework—that fateful homework—was to have a go at writing a poem in free verse. Mine, I remember, had images of icebergs and seals and polar bears frolicking and bounding on ice floes. I enjoyed writing it, and Miss H. gave me a good grade, making only one negative comment in the margin, which was that I ought not to have included penguins. (Either Miss K.'s geography lessons had not covered the differential fauna of the polar regions or my enthusiasm for poetry writing had overridden my knowledge of what animals lived at which pole.) I copied the poem into my private poetry book at home, leaving out the embarrassing reference to penguins.

My friend Ann had felt no such enthusiasm for the homework assignment. In fact, it had sent her into a blue funk. The rhyming stuff had been bad enough, but this new idea, this free verse thing, was worse. Having no idea what was required of her, Ann had turned to me in desperation. Naturally, I had been eager to help my friend. And writing poetry was such fun.

The day our homework was returned to us, Miss H. asked me to stay behind after the class.

My eyes were downcast throughout the short interview that changed my life.

Miss H. came straight to the point. "Ann didn't write her poem, did she?" she said softly. "You did."

I was speechless. How on earth could she have known?

"Every good writer," she explained, "develops his or her own style. It is as distinctive as a fingerprint. Normally, that style doesn't develop until a person is much older. It's very rare for someone as young as thirteen to have a clearly developed style. But you do."

I cannot remember now whether Ann or I or both of us were punished for our attempts to deceive. But somehow I suspect we were not. What purpose would it have served? Clearly, I could never do Ann's homework for her again, for now I knew that my writer's fingerprint would be set indelibly upon it. And I like to think that Miss H. considered Ann more in need of encouragement than of punishment.

Even had I been punished, the gift she had given me would have far outweighed the pain of it. For Miss H., in reprimanding me, had also baptized me. Suddenly I understood the rush of feeling that had come when I'd heard her read the poem. I, too, was a writer.

It is not easy to make a living from writing, and I only made one attempt at it. When I was eighteen, I applied for a position as an advertising copywriter with a large fashion house. I did not get the job. I went to work in a library instead. Later—much later, after my own children were at school—I went back to college and eventually became a psychologist.

One day, a local editor who knew I was running stress-management seminars asked me to write a short piece on stress-management for his paper. I happily agreed. It gave me quite a buzz to see my name in print. After that, I began to publish articles in magazines. I wrote stories, won some prizes, tried my hand at poetry again. At fifty-three, I published my first book. At sixty-six, I published the second one. Now officially retired, I write every day. I am more contented than I have ever been.

Not long ago at a meeting of our local writers' circle, there was a discussion about what constitutes a writer. Are you a writer simply because you love words and you love to write? Do you become a writer when you see your words in print? Are you a writer only once someone has paid you for your work?

"Well, there is no doubt about you," said one of my colleagues. "You are certainly a writer. Look at all the work you have published—books, articles, short stories, poems."

I smiled to myself. It took no books or articles to make me a writer, and it definitely did not take money. I have been a writer all my life, most certainly since I was thirteen. Miss H. told me so.

Oh, how I wish I could have thanked her—her and that snake.

~Marian Van Eyk McCain

I Remember Anna

I discover Anna Quindlen during a lunch hour in 1986. Every moment I am not working at my dreary college catalog–writing job, I spend reading. Her "Life in the 30s" column in the *New York Times* speaks to a particular group of women at particular points in their lives. She reveals everything I think and feel, wonder and rant about. Her beautifully written essays, so human, so gracefully crafted, are about serious topics and serendipity, fate and love, childhood memories and adult quandaries, and how it is all somehow bound up together. It reminds me why I wanted to write at all—and that I do not have the writing life I wanted. I want to write like Anna Quindlen. I probably want to be Anna Quindlen.

A few years later I am doing some freelance writing when not at my dreary public relations writing job, and an editor friend calls. He has a new job at an upstart regional magazine covering Hudson County, home to New Jersey's largest landfill, the embroidery capital of the United States, and Hoboken—where Sinatra first crooned, baseball was born, and Anna Quindlen lives and works.

"How would you like to interview Anna Quindlen?" Bill asks. Knowing I'll say yes, he doesn't wait for a reply. "She's on a book deadline now. So in the meantime, can you do Gene Heller?"

I spend an hour with the charming Mr. Heller, who, decades before, looked at the Hackensack River meadowlands and saw a sports-retail-business complex where others saw only swamp. Months pass. I write about embroidery and about the world's largest flush toilet research facility. The pay is decent and I need the work, but on each article submitted I scrawl, "What about Anna Q?"

Finally, the magazine arranges an interview. The anticipation is excruciating. I fantasize: She sees what I already know from her columns, that we have much in common—favorite movie (*Gone with the Wind*), Catholic school background, longing for a mother (hers dead; mine distant). After we bond, I ask her to read an essay I've written. You never know. And although I know it is a fantasy, I panic and think, *Now I must write an essay!* And I do, about postpartum depression, because it is personal and something I know.

The day before my scheduled interview with Anna Q., Bill's tight voice barks from my answering machine: "The magazine folded. The interview is off." *Bill is out of work but I do not care.* I do reflexively check to ensure that the magazine paid me for my last assignment.

It does not occur to me that I could have called Anna Quindlen and asked if I could come anyway, sold the interview to another publication, pushed my essay to her across the coffee table. You never know. Instead, I drop my essay into a drawer.

A year or two later, my friend Denise calls while I am writing a local business advertorial for my dreary job at a tiny newspaper. I welcome the distraction. She invites me to hear Anna Quindlen speak at an event two towns over. We go, love every minute, and afterward queue up for the book signing.

Denise is pregnant and hot. "I need air. But you stay," she offers. "Meet me at the car."

Of course I will stay. How could I not? I have waited so long for this, I have to tell her. . . . Tell her what? That we were going to meet once, but didn't? That I decided to write essays because of her, and yet, two years later, I still don't?

"Did you get to talk to her, or did she just sign?" Denise wants to know when I get to the parking lot.

"Neither," I say. "I'm tired of waiting. Let's go."

At home, I kiss my sleeping toddler, kiss my husband, who has fallen asleep watching the Yankees, go into my office and push the door closed. I find the essay; I edit and rewrite. Months later, it appears in the *Big Apple Parent's Paper*, not exactly a top-tier journalism venue. Still, it's my essay, and I think it speaks to a particular group of women about an especially poignant time in their lives.

~Lisa Romeo

Talking on Paper

"W hy I Should Not Talk in Class"—the title was the easy part. How on earth was I going to write a five-page essay on that, even with my big, loopy, fifth-grade scrawl? I was a straight-A student, so I knew the wisdom of listening in class, and my punishment had taught me that it wasn't a good idea to get on my teacher's last nerve. But five pages? That would take all night!

I was always timid. Being new to the school made me even shyer, so it was surprising I'd chat to anyone around me, especially to a boy. Fate must have pushed me to blurt out a comment, I can't remember what, to Roger that day. Now I was paying a hard price.

The school bus took forever getting home. How would I finish my essay and show my face at school tomorrow? Once I got home, though, I took my time petting the cat and drinking a soda—postponing the pain.

When I finally sat down to write, I began with the predictable reasons I knew Miss Jeter would want to hear. Talking kept me and my neighbors from learning. One paragraph down; now what? I chewed on my pencil. Aha! What if all that talking went uncorrected? What if talking were the first rude step toward life as a criminal? My lawless future opened before me as I jotted it down. Without the education I was throwing away, I'd have no opportunity. I'd turn to theft, armed robbery, and go to prison. When I got out, friends and family would scorn me. Strangers on the street would point a finger and say, "See that ex-con. She used to talk in class." The pages began flying by.

But when Mama got home from work, I was still complaining, "Five pages! That's impossible!"

"Well, you'd better get back to work," she said, "and I want to read it when you're through."

Ouch! Why couldn't I shut up?

After dinner, I wrote the last page and handed the essay to Mama. I half expected a lecture—at least an, "I hope you've learned your lesson." Instead, Mama laughed and laughed as she read, until tears rolled down her face. Then she attached her own note to the essay: "Dear Miss Jeter, I'd like this essay back when you've finished with it."

The next day, the usual knot in my stomach before facing my new class was so huge I had trouble eating breakfast. After roll call, Miss Jeter asked if we had our essays. Roger and I passed them in. As we sat working math problems, my stomach began to calm down. Then Miss Jeter announced, "Class, I'd like to read Alarie's essay to you."

I felt my cheeks burn as everyone turned to stare at the once invisible new kid. She read. They laughed. They all laughed! And I could tell they weren't making fun of me: They laughed because I had the power to tell a funny story. I didn't feel so much like an outsider any more. Kids even came over at recess to talk to me.

Did I decide that day to become a writer? No, my confidence still needed some nudging, but I did learn that I wasn't quiet and shy in print. Later, I wrote for the school paper. I wrote when I was angry or frustrated. I wrote for my own amusement. But when grownups asked, "What do you want to be when you grow up?" I shrugged.

With my continuing good grades, Mama told me, "You can do anything you set your mind to." I wanted to think so, but few women I knew worked, and my own family strongly favored the science and math track pursued by my older brother. My love of painting was encouraged only as a hobby, and I wasn't convinced I had a future in writing. Little did I know the choice of a single class would decide my college major and my vocation.

My high school offered various accelerated classes during a five-week, all-day summer school for gifted students. I selected creative writing. My favorite English teacher, Mr. Wheeler, taught the class, which included weekly field trips and a weekly tutorial by a professor from the College of William and Mary. Now, who else would turn up in that class but Roger from the fifth grade. During our introductions, he told the others, "You should have heard Alarie's essay on why not to talk in class!"

Mr. Wheeler responded, "I didn't know she could talk for the first six months she was in my class."

I was pleased to have an advocate in Roger, since I still hadn't learned to speak up for myself. Besides that, he and two of the other guys called themselves poets and walked around quoting Shakespeare, Eugene O'Neill, and writers I'd never heard of. I was in awe—plus a little jealous of how they hung out together and supported each other. I couldn't even understand what they were writing half the time, but believed the lack was in me.

Our class went to see the adaptation of a Molière play at a dinner theater, about which we were required to write a review. I held my breath as the college professor strolled in for the first time to critique us. He put one of the poet's papers on an overhead projector and read—blah, blah, blah, long words I couldn't understand, but assumed were profound. Then he said, "What the blazes does that mean?"

I was stunned. This professor had to be mighty tough to dismiss my idol's writing. Now I was even more afraid of what he'd say about my naive observations. "Look what this writer tells us," he said as he popped my paper onto the screen. I slumped in my seat.

"There's just something funny about seeing people fall down," I'd written, and then proceeded to point out the universal appeal of the play.

"Now that is plain English and good writing," he said, when finished reading my essay.

I couldn't believe my ears! I sat up straight, even though I knew I was blushing. My teachers had always said, "Write what you know." Here was proof it worked.

And that was the moment I knew I was a writer—had always been a writer—and now wanted to become a better one. Someday, I imagined, people could point to me and say, "See that writer? She used to talk in class."

~Alarie Tennille

Bountiful Hunger

In 1980, the poet Phyllis Koestenbaum published *Hunger Food* (Jungle Garden Press), which chronicles the angst and secret life of the author's coming of age in Brooklyn and the cuisine that fueled it. The book's emotional and tactile imagery has resonated with me for two decades. "The belly lox skin is mine," Phyllis writes. "White, it has a little tender lox left, I scrape the lox off with eager teeth."

Not unlike a multitude of other citizens of the Nation of Storytellers, I sit down at my keyboard each morning to write. I cannot write on an empty stomach and sometimes blame Phyllis's book of poems for this shortcoming. After inhaling a bowl of rice crisps into which I have chopped a banana dusted with soy powder and soaked with vanilla-flavored soymilk, I can at least try to write. On a full stomach I write about the empty stomachs of Northwest pioneers, or about their possibly black and empty hearts, their barren fields, their barns just leveled by cyclones. I use the verb "to write" here advisedly. Sometimes I may sit in front of my computer screen for hours and type only one line or one sentence.

Mid-morning, I feel an emptiness coming on. I re-write my line or sometimes delete it entirely. The emptiness begins to echo. Trekking downstairs, I search the kitchen for baked Brie, double chocolate-almond torte, French bread drizzled with pressed garlic soaked in extra virgin olive oil and balsamic vinegar.

Two years ago I embarked on a life of health and fitness, so of course I do not eat these things, but I still look for them and, like a lost beloved, think about them constantly. The comfort of rice pudding dotted with succulent sweet yellow raisins comes to mind. The way the raisins pop between my molars, the way the custardy pudding oozes between my tongue and jaw, then slides down the back of my throat. The chewy, cinnamony scum stretched across the top of the blue baking dish encases a flavor enhanced by sweet unsalted butter. The taste of butter has not passed my lips for two consecutive winters.

I heat some water in the microwave, into which I float a mint tea bag. If I feel really motivated, I'll go outside into the raging Cascade mountain wind and pick some of the now frozen mint that grows by the water faucet next to the house, pulling the leaves off the vine like fish scales, and then pour hot water over them. Hot-coal-of-a-cup in hand, I return to my desk and try to write about Virginia Reed and her desperate parents in the winter of 1847 in the high Sierras existing on pine needle soup made from melted snow. I picture her entertaining the elders of the Donner party with food rhymes on a feastless Christmas Eve. I imagine the Reeds regretting their hunger for land and a new life in California and wonder what forms their regret took.

Sipping my tea, I recall that once, inspired by Phyllis Koestenbaums's *Hunger Food*, I tried to write a villanelle that consisted solely of food I would eat if I could eat anything I wanted to, nonstop. The last two words of the first (and often repeated) line were "Brie cheese." The poem failed to fly, not because of any lack of passion for Brie on my part but because of my inability to find enough mouth-watering foods that rhymed with "cheese."

What is it we hope for when we write? Many things, of course, but one of which might be that the sum of the ingredients, the elements of narrative, say—characterization, plot, point of view, setting, theme—in the end add up to be more than the sum of the story's parts. Not unlike what we hope for when we make cheese or bake bread. Brie is more than milk and the lining of a cow's stomach, and bread is more than flour, water, and leavening. The cheese I imagine is gooey, with salty fat globules melting across the tongue. My teeth tear the bread's crust like meat; the chewy center's flesh leaves a tangy aftertaste. Together, these Biblical foods have the capacity to lift our spirits, to fill our heads with new ideas and possibilities, to comfort us; whereas cheese and bread's pre-dough components have none of these capabilities. Good bread is genius; flour/water/yeast is not.

Good writing is in some ways like good cooking. It takes inspiration, energy, devotion, discipline, and a spark of obsessive human emotion possibly bordering on insanity. It takes not just the right ingredients, but also a sense for flavor, a flair for inventive substitutions. Rising time, baking, cooling, and aging time all become inspired transitions. In the end, the life of a citizen of the Nation of Storytellers boils down to this:

We cook, we break bread, we write, we hunger. We write some more.

~Jana Harris

This essay was first published under the title "Remembering Brie" in the online poetry journal *Switched-on Gutenberg*, December 28, 2001.

Confessing in 5,000 Steps

Last summer I vowed to start walking every day. Of course, I'd write every day; that had about the same priority as breathing, eating, and sleeping.

I write confessions for a living. My normal output is cranking out one short story a week. It could be a mini-story of 1,000 words, or it could be a regular length of 5,000 words. No matter. The point is, I must come up with one story per week. It's just the way things are.

Walking is an addictive sport, and I don't question that it is a sport. You don't need any fancy uniform to prove it's a legitimate sport; you just put on some sturdy shoes and off you go. At first, of course, you huff and puff along, not venturing too far from your front porch. You baby-step a few minutes, as you try to take note of the scenery along the way, and you try not to complain about how your knees ache.

Each day you walk a few steps farther. You find yourself setting informal goals. Maybe I can make it to that pine tree or to the next fork in the road. You're on your own, because nobody's pushing you to keep at it. There's no cranky editor urging you to hurry up.

As time progressed, I realized walking and writing don't mix well for me. I'd be spending so much time outdoors in the fresh air, making tracks on the dirt roadway, that I wasn't spending enough hours working at my computer. I have no other job. Freelancing is what puts food on our table, so it's important I stick to my goal of sending out one short story each and every week, come rain or come shine.

In my walking world, blocks had soon turned to miles, and I was hardly griping about my sore knees any more, even though I was covering greater distances. I had to get up a little earlier to start my walks, because I was gallivanting all over the countryside. Sometimes I took the dogs with me, other times not. By October, I was outdistancing them anyway.

By the time I got home each afternoon, it would be time for lunch. Then I had a few fast hours at the computer before it was time to start cooking dinner. My work output was suffering drastically. It seemed impossible to write the 5,000-word stories anymore. I'd struggle to get to 1,000 and then call it quits. The trouble was, a few editors wanted 10,000-word confessions. I didn't seem to have enough hours in my day anymore. What was I going to do?

A notebook is a writer's friend, or so I've heard. It's perfect when you're watching TV and want to jot down a few brilliant ideas. It's a fine tool for that time spent waiting in bank or grocery store lines. The ideas just seem to leap out onto the paper. But a notebook is of little value when you're on the trail and on the move, I discovered. My writing output had decreased, and I was stymied.

I asked writer friends for advice, but they had no solutions. Either quit walking or quit writing, they told me. Some help that was! I started carrying a portable cassette recorder on my daily jaunts. At first I was too shy to speak into the thing. Face it, it looked silly. Or nutty. Blazing the trail and talking to myself. Or worse, talking to a trio of dogs.

I had the recorder with me for a solid week before I uttered a single word. "Testing," I whispered into the built-in microphone. It wasn't a very remarkable start. It wouldn't launch me anywhere near 5,000 words, let alone 10,000. Not even a mini-confession of 1,000 words.

Where were my words about women afraid of new romantic entanglements, about teens fighting drugs, about grandmas in love? What I needed was a way to get the short-story plots from my head onto cassettes, later to appear on my computer screen. But who wants to walk past chicken coops or olive groves talking into a little plastic machine? It doesn't feel natural.

"Try changing your approach," my best friend, Charlene, told me. "Just pretend you're on the phone with me. Gossip. Tell me every sordid detail."

Oh, what a genius that Charlene is!

Every day I hike past intricately plowed fields, up steep pathways better designed for mountain goats than humans, along pine-lined trails. I tell Charlene details about bitter marriages, giving up babies for adoption, about troubles with bickering in-laws. Our world is chock-full of heartbreak, and it's my job to illustrate these problems for the reading public. I can open up to Charlene about anything. The lies, the deceit, the tears. The smiles, the reunions, the unexpected happy endings. If it's pouring rain, the relationships might turn stormy. If it's sunny, love might prevail.

"Next the hero said . . ." and "then the protagonist answered . . ." The dialogue comes spurting out of me. The plots weave surprising patterns, often as twisty as my walkways. On and on I trek, baring my soul, opening up my imagination, paying attention to my surroundings, uncovering secret after secret, creating sentences out of words, paragraphs out of sentences. Mile after mile, page after page. Walking gives me the perfect working rhythm. Friends have asked if I ever want to take up running. No way! My stories might run clear off the pages.

I walk and I talk, period. That's what I do. That's how I work. Once I get started, I can gab to Charlene for hours about anything and everything that pops into my head. Later, at my computer, my final task is to squeeze out the best stuff and to take out whatever doesn't belong in the story. Some of the taped words fit the storyline, others don't. The completed stories get transmitted from my computer to editors. From there, they make it onto pages of *True Romance,* or *Black Confessions,* or *Bronze Thrills,* or *True Confessions,* or *Jive.*

As my walks became longer, I noticed that my resulting stories did too. These days, I rarely submit a 1,000-worder. That would be a walk around the block. Kid stuff. I view 5,000 words as my starting point. The sky's the limit. As long as my battery supply holds out to keep the recorder going and I don't get laryngitis, I'm confessing for the long haul.

~*Roberta Beach Jacobson*

Time Enough

June 16, 2006: Early

It's 6:30 on a Friday morning. My seven-year-old son, Ryan, who is prone to stomach problems, is nauseous and lying on the family room floor, while my husband, Greg, who is prone to inner ear problems, is dizzy and lying on the kitchen floor. The day has just taken off, and already it's hiccupped and spun, crashed and burned, pinning all of my plans—for a manic morning of errands and then a quiet afternoon of writing—beneath it.

I get Ryan onto one couch, Greg onto another, and my daughter, Alaina, off to school. After Greg assures me that he'll listen for Ryan's cry (although he can't promise he'll be able to actually help him), I speed off to Home Depot. It's almost Father's Day and the Shop·Vac sale ends today.

But when I get to the store, the vacuum I'd reserved over the phone has mysteriously disappeared (of course it has!), and there are no more like it (of course there aren't!). The men "helping" me amble off with vague promises to keep looking, while I wander the aisles alone, comparing serial numbers on the shelves with the one on my slip of paper. I finally find one and carry the big, awkward box to the counter, where I wait in one line to pay and then in another to get the rebate form. After fiddling with the printer for several minutes, the clerk tells me that it needs more toner (of course it does!) and asks why I can't just print the form at home. I say I can, resisting the urge to tell her I could have been home already, doing just that.

I race through two more errands—Safeway for bread and juice, the post office to mail a late bill. On the drive home, I daydream about getting me and my two sick guys upstairs to our big king bed, where, with any luck, we'll all sleep this wreck of a day away.

1961–1994

I'm a painfully shy girl who cares more for books than for Barbies or baby-sitting—a geek who dreams of being abandoned and then adopted by her real family: Alcott and Jo March, Dickens and David Copperfield. After surviving high school, I escape two hours north to the

University of Washington, where I major in English and technical writing, begin dating, and start shedding my insecure snakeskin of a self.

Life after college gets even better. While working as a technical writer and making more money than I ever thought possible, I take creative writing classes at night and publish two nonfiction stories. One editor asks me to write a regular column ("Something à la Anna Quindlen," he says), but I turn him down: Quindlen is a mother, after all, and middle class going on middle age. We have nothing in common.

Meanwhile, I marry Greg, and we honeymoon in Spain. He starts a business I agree to help with, and we buy a tiny bungalow in a north Seattle neighborhood, which we pretend to "keep" (neither of us knows how to cook or clean). We watch subtitled movies and read serious novels and then go to artsy coffeehouses to talk about what we just saw and read. Greg is a singer and I'm a writer, and we hang out with architects and dancers, massage therapists and painters.

Only we're so busy making money and hanging out with artsy people that we don't actually have time to sing or write. I don't write for a month, then six. I don't worry about this because for me, time is still on time, fanning out into infinity.

1995–2001

We have a daughter, Alaina—something so jarring that it precipitates a move to the suburbs and the purchase of a minivan—and I quit my technical writing work. Greg starts another business and a new job, and Alaina starts having night terrors the day I bring her brother, Ryan, home from the hospital. I start nothing. I go to bed at 11:00 P.M., get up with both children alternately throughout the night, and then get up with Ryan for good at 5:00 A.M. If sleep is like "little slices of death," as Edgar Allan Poe said, I must be saving up for the whole loaf all at once. I wonder if it's something I can order on the Internet.

I've always gotten my energy from being alone, and without this time—to read and write, to assimilate my last social encounter and rev up for the next—life is flat, relentless, blinding. My children bloom in the hothouse of family life, while I wither. Tiny pieces of respite melt into mirage and then disappear.

I try to distract myself with things I can do without thinking—home businesses, shopping, drinking—and when a new neighbor gushes, "What's not to like about the suburbs?" I feel guilty. Who am I to be unhappy when I have everything so many women want?

January 2002

One day while Alaina is in school and Ryan is watching cartoons, I pull out an old journal and read about a class I took in 1988: "Met Ted and Bharti today; I guess we'll be critiquing each other's work. Also met Shannon, who introduced herself with haiku:

I was a writer / And then I had my daughter / Ten years, more, have passed."

I have that out-of-body sensation where I'm hovering over my own life, and I watch myself scanning Ted's movie reviews over the years and passing my hand over Bharti's culinary novels at the bookstore. I see how quickly ten years pass and how it's possible for anything, even haiku, to turn into epitaph. Mostly I see how the infinite fan of time, as deftly as if it were in the hands of a practiced geisha, eventually turns its back on everyone.

2002–2005

I turn forty, and the desire to write again gets tangled up with the desire to hold on to what's left of my youth. I spend afternoons, while Ryan is in preschool, sitting in front of a blank screen one minute and standing in front of the bathroom mirror the next. How can something that feels so smooth look so wrinkled? I daydream about seducing both the writing muse and the clerk at the liquor store.

I plan to meet two college acquaintances for dinner. Then I walk by their table several times, because I don't recognize in them the young girls I remember.

When I finally start writing, it takes me six months to "finish" an essay and then another six to whittle it down to slivers and cobble it back together again. I take a writing class online and get responses that fall into one of three categories: This is too depressing! I love your writing! Are you writing a book?

I send an essay to a journal, trying not to think about 700 writers (or 7,000) competing for seven acceptances. And always I tell myself, as a vaccination against grief, not to expect too much, that my love of writing may go unrequited.

September 2005

For the first time, both of my kids are in school all day. I fantasize about going to lunch with friends, keeping a perfect house, exercising and exfoliating myself back to ten years ago, all while writing pithy essays, but this isn't Sex and the Suburbs. This is real life, and I'm a slow writer, and if I'm really going to do it, I'll have to ignore most other things.

I take another writing class online, pore over journals and magazines, and send out more writing.

When friends find out what I'm doing, they lower their voices and ask, "Well, what kind of things do you write?"—as if I've just admitted to committing a crime and they're trying to figure out how much trouble I'm in.

November 2005

Ryan points to the Modern Library editions on my shelves and asks about the pictures on them: Dostoevsky, Faulkner, Welty. "One day, you'll be on a book," he says solemnly, and I'm ruined for the rest of the day. He still believes that Alaina will be Kelly Clarkson and he'll be Ichiro; that his mother will somehow be transformed into the visiting author at Sierra Heights Elementary.

January 2006

I read about a woman whose essay was rejected thirty-two times before being published and then chosen for a Best American Essays anthology. When I start getting my own rejections, I try to feel glad.

I sign up for a feature writing class to make my writing more marketable, but I'm afraid of the phone and never get around to interviewing anyone. Besides, I'm on this roller coaster for one reason only—love—and I know deep down that I'm only going to write what I want to write. I drop the class.

March 2006

I stumble upon writer Lynn Freed's scathing story in *Harper's* about writing students and her life as a teacher. Even though she isn't my teacher, I'm both angry and embarrassed. Who is she to think I can't write? Who am I to think I can?

Some of the rejections I get are ruthless, while some are mildly encouraging. After a fellow classmate laments that he's gone from counting his rejections to stacking and measuring them, I'm careful to keep mine in separate folders.

May 2006

"Meet me at the palace at 4:00 sharp. Call if you need a different time. Speak of this to no one. Bring only one person, if you must. Signed, The Prince"

I find this note Alaina wrote for a game, and it makes me laugh. It's all there: the need to have secrets and to share, to acquiesce but give up no ground, to stand alone and bring someone along. It occurs to me that the paradoxes in writing are the same as in life; that writing, for me, is life.

June 16, 2006: Noon

What I actually do when I get back from Home Depot is this: feel foreheads, get glasses of water, load the dishwasher, print the rebate form, check e-mail. And there it is, the news I've tried not to hope for: "Thank you for your submission; we like it very much." I run out to the couch to tell Greg I'm going to be published. As he gets up to hug me, lunging through his spins, I feel as giddy as a teenager, in love with the world because it loves her back.

August 18, 2006

The magazine I'm to be published in doesn't come out until September, but a friend calls to tell me that a teaser for it has been posted on the magazine's Web site. It's fun news on an otherwise hard day: Greg and I have been to see an attorney, because our latest business is failing and may take our personal finances down with it.

Back when I had all the time in the world to write—before the responsibilities of children and a home, before the realization that I, too, would eventually grow old—I just didn't seem to have much to say. Back then I wrote what little I did because I could, not because I couldn't keep it in.

Now that I've lived long enough to learn that nothing can make me immune—to age, to loss—I take great pleasure in this simple fact: that for this moment I have a lot to say and, despite the wolves at the door, time enough in which to say it.

~Lorri McDole

The Write Mother

I'm a woman," I informed my mother. "You're sixteen," she corrected.

"I'm a writer," I insisted.

"Yes," she agreed, "you are a writer."

"Then why do I have to stay behind each year while you go to the women's writing conference? Why can't I go too?"

When most teenagers begged their mother to let them spend the summer at the beach with friends (and away from prying parental eyes), I pleaded with mine to take me away for a week with her to the International Women's Writing Guild's annual summer conference. When most mothers insisted that their daughters focus on less artistic and more practical career goals, my mother granted my request. So on a rainy August morning in 1987, we loaded the car, headed west on the Massachusetts turnpike, and journeyed to the campus of Skidmore College in Saratoga Springs, New York.

As we turned into the entrance of our destination, Mom revealed that she had arranged separate rooms for us. "This is my vacation," she informed me. "I need my space. I'll give you the lay of the campus and we can sit together during meals in the cafeteria, but other than that, you're on your own. Take workshops or don't. I don't care. Just remember that you wanted to come, so make the most of your stay."

My initial shock of Mom's sudden declarations left an unsteady feeling in my stomach. Even though I attended boarding school during the academic year and was used to being responsible for getting myself up and where I needed to be, I certainly didn't expect my mother to try ditching me moments upon arriving at the conference site. I was also unprepared to see my mother act like a teenage girl returning to summer camp as she squealed and hugged friend after friend. Who were all these women? Who was my mother? What had I gotten myself into?

"This is my daughter, Judy," Mom announced with pride several times an hour. "She's a writer too."

"Oh, how lucky you are to have such a wonderful relationship," the other woman would gush, followed by, "My daughter doesn't like to write," or "My daughter wouldn't dare spend a week with me."

A mere four hours later, I was completely caught off guard when my mother, who had been content to let me fend for myself, grabbed my arm and charged us up on to the opening ceremony stage. There I stood in front of five hundred women with Mom's arm wrapped tightly around my shoulder, on display as one of the Guild's few mother/daughter teams in attendance. Was my mother insane? Since when had we become the epitome of the mother/daughter relationship? Sure, we both liked to write. But she was an overprotective mother, and I was an overemotional teenager; we hardly deserved an auditorium full of applause.

"I can't believe you just did that," I whispered when we sat back down.

"I know."

"That was so embarrassing."

"I know."

"It was humiliating and mortifying."

"Someone's been working on her vocabulary."

"Oh, never mind!"

The next morning I was more than happy to be on my own. No longer a showpiece for Mom's ego, I left my room in search of a playwriting workshop. Mom didn't write plays, so I knew she wouldn't go to that class. Unfortunately, I completely underestimated the complexity of the Skidmore campus layout and the vagueness of the campus map. As I stood in the center of the quad, searching for a point of reference, a kindly voice asked, "Hi, Judy. Need some help?"

Taken aback, I rudely replied, "Do I know you?"

"No, but I'm friends with your Mom. Which workshop are you going to?"

"Playwriting, but I can't find the Learning Center building."

"The Learning Center is actually in the Tisch building, right over there. I'm headed that way too. Come on."

As I entered my chosen classroom another stranger waved me to her. "Over here, Judy! Your mom said you'd probably come to this class, so I saved you a seat."

As the week progressed, I realized that showing me off to all her writing colleagues had less to do with her pride and more to do with my growth as both woman and writer. Like any good mother, Mom knew what made me tick. She understood that if I entered a room of strangers, my shyness would get the best of me. I'd listen intently, take copious notes, but remain quiet. Yet she also knew that if I sat among people I knew, I'd be much more outgoing. I'd speak up, share my work, and give feedback to others. Tossing me into the cold water of public recognition during that first opening ceremony, Mom knew her fellow Guild friends would act as lifeguards, helping me keep my head above water as I learned to swim on my own. More important, she'd tossed me in, having the undeniable faith that I could swim.

Fourteen years later, I grabbed Mom's arm and pulled her on to the opening ceremony stage. Although we had attended the Guild's conference together during some of the intervening years, this time we were being recognized as the only mother/daughter workshop leaders in attendance. Where once I had stood wanting to melt into nothing, I now stood proudly with my arm wrapped around Mom and grinning from ear to ear. I looked out into the audience of women, many of whom had become significant writing mentors in my life, and silently acknowledged them with a nod. And as I squeezed Mom's shoulder, I realized that I no longer stood as a child with her mother. I now stood as a writer with her greatest mentor, a mentor who had provided countless other teachers. I stood as a published author with the "write" mother.

~Judy L. Adourian

The Only Cure for the No-News Blues

A year ago I discovered there was something worse than a rejection slip: not hearing anything at all. But I was to learn even that may not be all bad.

Having finished what I thought was the final draft of my novel, I made an appointment to see an agent at a writers' conference in a quaint hotel on the Oregon Coast. It would be a perfect place to pamper my muse and gather the courage to pitch my book.

I'll call the agent Amy. She looked like an Amy—sweet, attractive, friendly. I liked her immediately. When I pitched my book to her, she smiled big and gushed, "Yes, please, send me three chapters and a query letter."

I was elated. This was my big chance.

Not wanting to rock the boat before I got into it, I humbly asked, "How long will it be before I hear from you?"

"I usually get an answer out in four to six weeks, sometimes sooner."

Sweet, likable Amy and I would be partners!

When I returned home, my husband, Dan, and I went out to dinner to celebrate.

It was April. On May 15th we were leaving on a month-long trip. I worked feverishly polishing the first three chapters so I could get the package out to Amy before I left. I wrote and rewrote, received supportive critique from my writers' group, and rewrote again. The night before we left, Dan rushed the query and first three chapters to the post office while I packed my stuff. I slipped a copy of the printed manuscript into my carry-on in case Amy e-mailed me asking to see the whole book—just in case I'd be one of those early recipients of sweet Amy's response.

While we were away, I checked my e-mail every few days with the anticipation of a mouse waiting for the cat to go to sleep, but I heard nothing from Amy while I was gone. When I returned home, I retrieved my snail mail from the post office and quickly thumbed through it. Nothing from Amy. I smoothed my disappointment; it had been only a month.

After eight weeks had passed without hearing from Amy, I e-mailed her stating I had sent the three chapters and the query letter she'd requested and asking her to please let me know if she had received them. Still, I heard nothing from her.

Then one day I had the strange feeling that in my rush to get the items mailed, I might have failed to enclose an SASE. That must be why I haven't heard from her, I rationalized. I sent another e-mail explaining I'd forgotten to send the self-addressed stamped envelope and told her I would send one, which I did posthaste.

A few more weeks went by. Trips to the mailbox left me empty-handed, and most of my e-mails were forwards ending with "have a nice day," which didn't help, because I knew I wasn't going to. Meanwhile, I had quit writing and discovered jigsaw puzzles. But I couldn't delete dear, sweet, unanswering Amy from my mind.

After six months crawled by, I called her.

Imagine my surprise when I heard a strange voice say, "This is Sally Something. Amy Amiable is out of the office for two weeks on vacation. I will be taking her calls. Please leave a message, and I'll make sure Amy receives it as soon as she returns." I left a message asking Amy to call me. I didn't hear from either one of them.

I vented to my critique group. "Even if she does contact you," they echoed, "don't hire her. She doesn't follow through. She's unprofessional. Forget about her."

I tried to take their advice, but thoughts swirled

through my head: *Why hadn't I heard from her? What did I do wrong? What could I do to make it right?* I was like a child whose parents were going through a divorce, blaming myself for what had happened.

My eyes opened a bit when I did a follow-up visit to my doctor for a sinus infection that wouldn't go away. "How are you doing?" she inquired.

"I'm still having headaches," I said.

"Does this hurt?" she asked, as she pushed on my facial sinuses.

"No, that part's better, I guess."

She looked in my ears and throat. "Are you still having yellow drainage? Any blood?"

"No, that seems to be cleared up."

She looked at me thoughtfully. "I don't think your headaches are sinus-related. I think they might be migraines."

Already at the edge of a bleak canyon, that statement pushed me over the side. I began to cry.

She took my hand. "What's wrong, Valetta, what's going on?"

"I don't feel good," I squealed.

"People usually don't cry just because they don't feel good," she said. "You seem pretty down in the dumps."

"I'm down in the dumps because I don't feel good."

"Is there something unpleasant going on in your life right now?"

My mom had died the year before, and I knew she was still on my mind a lot. And, of course, there was Amy, and because of Amy my book was in limbo, but I didn't feel like rehashing all of that with the doctor. Like a lot of people who don't write, she'd probably blow it off, or worse yet, laugh.

"No," I squeaked.

"I think you would benefit from an SRI." I knew what that was, a tactful term for an antidepressant. "Try it for six months," she said.

I left her office telling myself I wasn't going to fill the prescription. How could I be depressed just because I hadn't heard from Amy Amnesia? But driving home I thought about my life. I was down in the dumps. I got out of bed in the morning thinking how nice it was going to be when I crawled back in at night. I didn't even have the energy to do the thing I loved: write. "That's not normal," I admitted aloud. I filled the prescription.

I knew it would take several days, maybe even weeks, before the SRI kicked in, but having a professional put a name to my moping around seemed to also help my attitude. A few days later I woke up hearing a nagging voice in my head: Get up and look at your book, it said.

Look at it? I could look at it, I suppose. Looking doesn't mean I have to write.

After using the bathroom and before getting dressed, I pulled a large mailing envelope from the bookshelf. With curious fingers I tugged the printed manuscript out of the womb where it had been implanted for over nine months and began reading. The first three chapters comforted me, like seeing old friends.

Then I scanned the fourth chapter, and the fifth, and the sixth. Good grief! There were errors! Despair squeezed my chest. I'd have to move things around, rewrite and revise, tighten and trim.

Then relief washed over me. I was glad I hadn't sent out the rest of the book! It wasn't ready after all.

My fingers struck the keys, rebirthing my book and lifting my spirits. The more I wrote, the more I wanted to write. I pinned a note to my desk that says: "You'll feel better if you write."

And Amy? As I wove words into silken prose, she shrank smaller and smaller in my memory. Today, I can't even remember her full name.

~Valetta Smith

Charity Begins at My Keyboard

The only thing worse than chasing an elusive idea through the labyrinth of my mind and cornering it long enough to get it onto the page is knocking on the doors of total strangers and asking them for money. For the last five years, I've done both. I've pursued ideas as a writer and people as a door-to-door canvasser for the Kidney Foundation of Canada.

Why do I spend my time doing things that are so difficult? I write because it's in my soul; I canvass because it's in my genes—literally. I inherited a form of polycystic kidney disease from my father, so this particular cause is close to my heart as well as my kidneys.

My writing and canvassing techniques are strikingly similar—and serve as a bad example for writers and canvassers alike. Although I always begin with a strict schedule and the best of intentions, we all know what happens to good intentions. As for schedules, other tasks push their way through to the forefront, and suddenly I'm staring my deadlines in the face and the deadlines aren't blinking. In fact, they're sticking their tongues out at me and making a noise that sounds suspiciously like "nah-nah-nah-nah-nah."

In the case of writing, I end up working feverishly at 2:00 A.M. in a desperate attempt to finish an article or story and send it off to an editor. For canvassing, I can usually be found knocking on doors during the last weekend of March in the middle of a rainstorm, if I'm lucky, or a snowstorm, if I'm not. March, which is Kidney Month in Canada, can be a fickle weather month, but it's never good when I canvass. The day after I hand in my receipt book, the sun is always shining—a sort of cosmic raspberry.

A few years ago, I realized my reluctance to canvass was actually a great opportunity. Not for canvassing, but for writing. Since writing gurus are forever telling people to write about what they know, I decided to write an article titled "Confessions of a Reluctant Canvasser." After all, I was an expert in this field with several years of practice—pretty much all bad, but the gurus never said anything about the quality of knowledge. Mostly, though, sitting at my computer and wrestling an article into submission was another way to postpone having to go out and knock on doors. As usual, the article fought back, refusing to get onto the page.

I did my usual burning of the midnight oil, and after many hours of revision upon revision, I came up with what I hoped was a humorous account of my trials, tribulations, and singular lack of success as a fundraiser. I say "hoped," because I've learned through experience that what sounds incredibly funny to me at two o'clock in the morning may not sound half as funny to an editor at a more respectable hour.

As an afterthought, I added a postscript to the article noting that if enough people read the article and sent in contributions, I could give up canvassing for good. Then I sent the piece off on spec to the newspaper, not expecting an answer.

Three days later I got an acceptance, and the next weekend it was published.

I made a copy of the article and sent it to my mother. After she read it, she made about a thousand copies and distributed them to all her friends, relatives, and neighbors. Even though she denies it, I think she even stood on the street corner and handed them out to passersby, telling them the article was written by "my daughter, the writer."

I do know that she brought extra copies to the dialysis unit where my father was a patient and gave them to every doctor, nurse, or technician she could corner. Then she sat down and read it out loud to the patients who were undergoing treatment. Since dialysis patients are hooked up to a machine and can't move around freely, she had a captive audience.

Unfortunately, that wasn't the end of the story. While writing the article made me feel good, getting it published made me feel even better, and getting paid for it made me feel great, it still didn't replace my canvassing.

So, one cold, wet Sunday at the end of March, I headed out to my designated street. A week later, I handed my kit and receipt book to my area captain, happy to rest my knuckles from knocking on doors for another year. While I was relieved the canvassing was over, I was disappointed at the small amount I had collected. Kidney disease doesn't evoke the same feelings as cancer, famine, or homeless kittens. I can understand that. If it weren't for my father, I probably wouldn't be involved either. I'd be sitting in front of my computer, pretending I was thinking while I was actually playing solitaire.

A few months later, I received a letter from the Kidney Foundation, inviting me to attend the annual general meeting and awards ceremony. The letter was headed to the trash when a name popped out at me— my name—under "Awards for Outstanding Efforts" in their recent campaign. Since my canvassing had netted a grand total of eighty-five dollars, someone had obviously made a mistake.

I called the foundation and discovered it was not a mistake. For weeks after my article was published, readers had sent in donations, referring to my article or even clipping a copy of it to their checks. I was a hero—at least to the foundation and maybe my parents too.

As a humorist, I was used to making people laugh. But for the first time, I had written something that had a real effect on people, beyond a momentary guffaw. The pen might not always be mightier than the sword, but it can be pretty damn powerful. It was exhilarating—even better than getting paid for the article.

The day after the ceremony, I hung the framed award on my office wall. Now, every time I get discouraged or feel my writing doesn't matter, I look up at it and am reminded of what I accomplished and how generous people can be when they hear of a need.

I try to write every day. And I still canvass—reluctantly—every March.

P.S. If you want to help me stop canvassing, please send a donation to your local branch of the Kidney Foundation. Tell them Harriet sent you.

~Harriet Cooper

The Greatest Gig on Earth

Every year in January, the circus speeds into town on a sleek, shiny train. This is Circus with a capital C—dazzling lights, girls in tights, and elephants lumbering in time, trunk to tail. It was tradition for our family to go. As the boys turned from toddlers to teens, it was the one activity we could still enjoy together, where they would consent to be seen in public with their parents. We hadn't missed a year since the day my shiny new husband won the hearts of his two ready-made sons with a four-of-a-kind handful of tickets for seats right down front and a promise of free-flowing soft drinks and snack foods coated in sugar.

But this was a low-tide year when it came to cash flow. Downsizing dropped me right off the organizational chart at the company where I'd worked, and the prospects of heeding the ringmaster's call for "Moms and Dads, Boys and Girls, Children of All Ages" looked dim. I dreaded telling the kids we'd have to get by on memories until next year. The trouble with life lessons is that they come along when what you really need is money.

There had to be a way to enlist some temporary financial security. I had grand intentions of polishing my resume to a degree that would ensure me the shiniest job ever to hit the classifieds, but in the meantime, how was I to continue the elite and grandiose lifestyle that my job as a secretary in a manufacturing plant provided? A career in computer technology was out, as I was somewhat befuddled once the job description ventured past "off" and "on." Swimsuit modeling was out, as most of my post-working days involved quaffing sodas and downing Ho Hos.

I decided to write. Due to the unfortunate termination from my desk job, I had plenty of time to burn pencil lead. An English major in college, I had a fancy diploma adorned with impressive stickers hanging on the wall behind the door at home, some experience with newspaper work, mostly from high school, and a secret, neglected dream to see my name in a byline. I gussied up a corner of my living room with a tiny desk and a computer that was the electronic equivalent of stone tablets.

Thinking about writing is like considering winning the lottery. You don't get a chance at the million without buying a ticket, and buying one ticket doesn't greatly improve your chances of collecting a stack of gold bars to use for pocket change. You have to dedicate yourself to the cause and grit your teeth when someone else's byline banks the check. So I queried. I counted words. I committed serial commas.

Staying focused long enough to finish a project is no more difficult than climbing the northeast face of Mount Everest alone with a juice box and a bag of powdered doughnuts for supplies. Just as you settle into your chair with creative thoughts bursting from your brain like socks from an overpacked suitcase, life sends a sudden squall in the form of a crying baby, a spouse with vanishing car keys, or a tub with mildewed grout that needs a hearty scrub. As tempting as that grubby grout may appear, you must resist the urge to grab the nearest toothbrush and scrub until everything is so shiny that Mr. Clean would need to don protective clothing to enter your bathroom. Stay in your chair and write.

I hated to check the mail. It was hard enough to read the rejections, but downright insulting that I had to provide the envelope and postage to have them delivered to my door. One afternoon when I eased up to the mailbox and peeked inside, there was another one of the dreaded Self-Addressed Stamped Envelopes peering out at me from the stack of bills. I saved it for last. Better to peruse the overdue power bill than to read another note that said, "No way. No talent." I slit the envelope, opened the folded sheet, and peered down with one eye. It said "Yes." It said "Thanks." It was the most beautiful document I'd ever smeared with sweaty fingers. My first acceptance. I squealed so loud a cardinal on a nearby pine branch nearly lost its grip.

My story appeared in a national newspaper. It ran on their official Web site. I snuck peeks at it every day to admire my name. It was two months until the circus. Should I pay the power bill or act fast enough to get seats near the Wheel of Death? I hovered over the auditorium's Web site, studying the seating chart.

I politely waited the month their contract stated it might take to persuade the accounting trolls to release the money. I ate my weight in Raisinettes and fingernails. No check. I sent the accounting trolls a tentative note that stated payment would be welcome and I had no interest in devouring their young if we came to agreement. No answer. Television commercials for the circus showed huge tigers padding back and forth in reinforced cages. I sent another note with darker overtones. Although I could stomach troll children, no matter how gamey, if they were covered with jam and sprinkled with sugar, a financial settlement would be infinitely more agreeable to my wallet and my digestive system.

One glorious day, the type when Mother Nature confuses winter with early fall, the check arrived. I paraded into the kitchen holding it aloft like the ring girl showing round seven at a prizefight. A cheer went up.

We circused. We ate cotton candy until our eyeballs turned to spun sugar. We squealed at the Wheel of Death and clapped thunderously when the tiger trainer emerged from the beastly cage with arms and legs intact. It was a glorious night. Son Number Two, possibly the coolest teenager that ever sustained life on chocolate milk and pizza, announced, "Mom, this is the greatest show on Earth!"

I think about that check from time to time as I thumb through folders thick with galley proofs and rejection slips. It's a reminder of the good and magical power of the Wheel of Death and of the pride and self-confidence that comes with the determination to keep working until your dreams are as close as the contents of a clown car. And that lesson is worth more than a Ho Ho in the hand.

~Amy A. Mullis

Out of Dry Ground

K athryn Jane, you have the makings of a fine writer!"

Over the years, many English teachers have so encouraged me to set high goals for my life. Then, an especially perceptive teacher gave me *Root Out of Dry Ground*, by Argye Briggs. Set in the barren region I called home, it was a life-changing book. Once I had read about Chris Sanders and her struggles to overcome poverty and ignorance to become a teacher, there was no doubt as to what I would do with my life: I would teach and I would write. I yearned to inspire others as Argye Briggs had inspired me.

I did, eventually, become an English teacher. However, I soon filled a shoebox with rejection slips. Finally, putting away my dreams of becoming an author, I wrote only in secret for nearly two decades. Then, in middle age, I sent off one more story—as a peace offering to my mother. It was to be a Mother's Day surprise, an effort to bridge the growing chasm between us.

My younger sister had once described our difficult relationship with Mother: "Loving her is like snuggling up to a porcupine or prickly pear." Both our parents had dropped out of elementary school. They were very bright and loved to read, but their large, impoverished families needed all hands at work around the farm. Moreover, they still lived in a nineteenth-century culture in which education for farm children was neither an attainable nor a valued goal—at least not in our part of the Southwest.

As my sister and I worked our way up the academic ladder, earning a string of degrees, teaching school, climbing slowly into the middle class, we often felt we were leaving our parents behind in the previous century. Daddy took great pride in his "brainy" daughters, but Mother was ambivalent. Though she bragged on us to neighbors, she was also resentful. She felt we were secretly critical of her poor grammar. She "seen" things we saw and "heerd" things we heard. She checked books out of the "liberry" and watched smoke rise up our "chimley." Hers was the language of the southern mountains with overtones of Elizabethan English (which I didn't learn until she'd been gone for a decade).

Our visits home were always tense, for we "walked

on eggs" around Mother. When we tried to compliment her for anything, she said we were patronizing her. If we didn't praise her, she said we felt superior and didn't appreciate her struggles.

HomeLife was my mother's favorite magazine. She eagerly picked it up each month at church and read it from cover to cover. So I daydreamed of surprising her with a story about our family's adversities during the Depression. Finally, one winter night, I sat at the kitchen table and wrote "The Summer We Lived in a Chicken House," a nostalgic look at the year we moved from Galveston, Texas, back home to a farm in Oklahoma. My parents had worked long hours and saved enough to buy a small piece of land, but there was no house on the place. My father quickly constructed a ten-by-twelve-foot chicken house, with a slanted tin roof and dirt floor, and that was our home for three golden summer months while we helped Daddy build a small, two-bedroom house. In retrospect, I realize that summer was very difficult for my parents, but it was joyous for me—and the joy shone through in my story.

I closed the piece with gratitude to my parents for "the riches they gave to me, that summer we lived in a chicken house." *HomeLife* bought the story and published it in May 1962. I've never forgotten the look of radiant wonder on my mother's tired, worn face when I gave her an advance copy of the magazine. She ordered copies for all her brothers, sisters, and friends, and our stormy relationship became more tranquil. It seemed convincing proof of the healing power of words.

HomeLife published another of my stories, "Grandma's Blessed Assurance," in June of that year, and I thought my career as a writer was finally "taking off." But only rejection slips followed for the next few years, and once again, I gave up writing for nearly two decades.

Finding my "voice" again in the 1980s, I published a string of poems and dozens of stories in anthologies, professional journals, and national magazines. Many of them were memories of my mother. How I'd like to show her the letters from readers who say, "I love your mother!" Writing about her has given me the perspective, understanding, and compassion I'd needed and wished I'd had while she was alive. And our story has resonated with other mothers and daughters trapped in difficult relationships.

I wrote about her delectable hot rolls and how she kept the recipe secret, leaving it in her Bible for us to find after her death. (Cooking was the only area in which she felt confident she could surpass "my girls.") I told how she hid our "nest egg" in the oven. Like many Depression survivors, my parents never trusted banks after 1929. Forgetting the money, Mother had cooked a roast the next day and incinerated our years' savings.

I told how she practiced her Sunday school lessons down in the hen house. She was a gifted Bible teacher but nervous about pronunciation and grammar. Daddy always said our old dominicker hens knew more about the Bible than most Baptist deacons he knew. I wrote about her terror of tornadoes and how we spent innumerable spring nights in the storm cellar, the "fraidy hole." I told how she publicly challenged a visiting preacher who was not solidly pre-millennial in his theology.

Finally, I wrote about the car wreck in her seventieth year that left her in a coma for months and caused significant brain damage. We all took turns sitting with her during long months in the intensive care unit. After we returned to our classrooms to teach, Daddy remained constantly at Mother's side, teaching her to read again, to feed herself, and to walk. Three years into her slow recovery, my father collapsed and died from the strain of caring for her. Mother lived another twelve years in a kind of twilight zone, where only two memories were luminously clear: the story I wrote about the summer we lived in a chicken house and living in that chicken house.

~Kathryn Presley

The Deal

My prayer was this: Please don't let me cry.

For weeks before the writers' conference, I'd go to bed daydreaming that the editor evaluating my work would be thrilled, and then I'd fall asleep and slide into a nightmare where she hated it. I had visions of this woman either laughing at me hysterically when I showed up for the evaluation or berating me for ten minutes straight about wasting her time with my too-immature-to-be-believed prose. I'd wake up in a cold sweat, heart hammering, devising excuses to not go to the conference, thereby avoiding the shame of a disastrous critique. However, money is a great motivator, and I'd already paid both my registration fee and the evaluation fee.

Besides, writers are made of tough stuff—even we novices. We have to be in order to open up our guts and lay them out on a blank page for everyone to view and judge. Even those of us who write mostly fiction know that every story mirrors a piece of our real selves—often more than we'd like to admit. Consequently, anyone who writes and then gathers up the courage to put it out there for others to read must build up an extra layer of skin—one the consistency of rubber, since we are forever called upon to rebound. To rebound and do it all over again, hopeful that next time our work will be met with acceptance, if not praise, rather than rejection, or worse, ridicule.

So, night after night, I'd go to bed with a nocturnal vision of being recognized for my wordsmithing skills. I'd visualize my humble acceptance of the accolades falling on my shoulders like confetti at a New Year's Eve party, and my generous grace in encouraging other writers who had not yet reached their pinnacles of success. Then every night, the recurring nightmare of failure and shame would awaken me from a restless sleep.

In hindsight, it's curious that I never envisioned a middle ground—a normal critique with red marks and suggestions to improve my work, maybe even a few "atta-girls" for what I'd done right. No, in my imagination, the upcoming review was going to bring either dazzling success or humiliating failure. Brass ring or fall off the horse.

Why this particular critique held so much power over me wasn't immediately obvious. I have been writing since I could hold a pencil. I wrote a little prayer when my grandfather died, when I was only six. At eight, I had a poem published in our church newsletter. In middle school, I wrote a poem that my teacher criticized for my use of archaic words such as "tis" and "days of yore." I was so embarrassed I didn't show anyone my work for years. In retrospect, maybe that incident planted the seed of fear that still haunts me. Nevertheless, I kept writing all the way through childhood and throughout my adult life, and the file box under my bed grew thick with stories and poems.

It wasn't until I was a grandmother, though, that I actually got a job that included "writing" in the job description. They actually paid me for putting words on a page! Granted, it was writing nonfiction, the pay wasn't great, and I received no bylines for what I wrote, but I was happy spending my days writing short biographies from completed questionnaires. Well, most of the time I was happy. There was still an editor to contend with—someone who had been head of the communications department for more than twenty years. He had definite opinions about each word that went into the biographies, and he let me know them daily. The proofed copies came back looking as though my granddaughter had scribbled pictures on them with a fine red pen. At first I bristled, but gradually I learned to accept his corrections and the explanations he insisted on throwing in free. Gradually, I became a better writer, a more thoughtful writer. In time, I could actually see the black letters on the page when he returned my work. I'm still not sure whether he was proud of me when he found less to correct, or disappointed that he had taught me too well.

Eventually, I got the courage to attend a writers' conference. The first time, I had no clue what to expect, what to bring, or what to do. That first conference was baptism by fire. I did learn, though, that for a small fee I could have submitted the first fifteen pages of a manuscript to be critiqued by an editor or agent. I vowed that I would do that at the next conference.

A year later, I had completed only about thirty-five pages of the first draft of my "great American novel," but that didn't dissuade me from submitting the required fifteen pages—just to see if I was on the right track. I wondered what possessed me to do so. Surely, the other writers attending the conference would be literary geniuses, consummate pros with credits to prove it. Certainly among them would be a few undiscovered John Grishams and Nora Robertses.

Despite my conviction that I was way out of my

league, the spunky little Pollyanna side of me said, "Hey, I might not be terrible. Friends and family have always liked my stories. The church folks liked the ones I submitted to the quarterly magazine. That editor just might like what I wrote."

So, the night before I was to attend the conference, I went to the bargaining table with God. I would attend the conference and the evaluation with my head held high, and He would not let me cry in front of the editor. Deal. I could live with that.

The next morning an abundance of nervous energy did a number on every part of my body. I paced back and forth, in and out of the bathroom, jaw clenched, shoulders hunched to the ears, stomach burning, breath catching. Somehow I managed to get myself ready, and I drove to the college in the next town. Trying to look cool and relaxed, I checked in and picked up my registration packet, which included a notice for my critique: 10:30 A.M., Room 212, Susan Mary Malone. I must have read it thirty times. Checking the map in my welcome package, I found the consultation room and the best way to reach it. I was ready . . . sort of.

I attended the first session, struggling to focus on the speaker's words while taking notes and glancing at the clock every fifteen seconds. At 9:45, I decided to leave the session and walk up the short flight of stairs to the critique room on the second floor. No need to wait until the last minute. After all, someone might collapse on the stairs in front of me, making me late for my 10:30 appointment. One couldn't be too careful in these situations. Besides, I needed to hit the restroom first; nervousness and too much coffee were taking their toll on me. I smoothed my hair, put on a touch of fresh lipstick, and reminded God of our deal.

I headed upstairs, forcing myself to take deep breaths so I wouldn't hyperventilate. Rounding a corner near the evaluation center, I ran into a friend of mine coming back from her critique with a different editor. She was not happy.

"How did it go?" I asked, already knowing from the scowl on her face that she had not been asked to sign a three-book deal nor given a six-figure advance.

"Not good. I should have picked a different editor to judge my work. This guy is interested only in crime novels. What does he know about real literature?"

"I'm sorry," I said, and meant it.

"Well, let's hope your person is kinder to you," she said.

I hoped so too.

I arrived at the manuscript evaluation check-in

station. The volunteers were people I had met early that morning over coffee.

"Nice to see you. Are you checking in for your evaluation?" Elizabeth asked.

"Yes, but I'm so nervous. I'm not sure I can do this," I confided.

"Oh, everyone feels like that, but it will be all right. Editors are people just like you. They actually want you to succeed. I'm sure the editor will be kind, whatever her thoughts about your story."

"Well, just so she doesn't make me cry."

It's not that I'm a crybaby by nature. It's just that my writing was very important to me. Something I loved to do. And I'd waited a long time to pursue my long-held dream of writing and publishing a novel. If the editor hated my first chapter, I didn't know whether I'd have the confidence or courage to complete the book. Standing there waiting for my turn, that thick skin of rubber completely melted away; I felt naked and exposed. Vulnerable.

The door to room 212 opened, and a man walked out, smiling back at Mrs. Malone as he left. *Okay, she didn't leave any marks on him,* I thought. *Maybe she's in a good mood from reading his amazing bestseller that will earn him big bucks and advance her career. She probably thinks my poor little attempt pales in comparison.*

I looked for another restroom.

"Just go on in," Elizabeth prodded from the registration table.

Taking a deep breath and holding to my deal with the Big Guy, I entered the room.

An attractive blond woman stood up and held out her hand to shake mine.

"You must be Susan Davis. I cannot tell you how happy I am to meet you!"

Me? I looked around to see if there might be someone else in the room. Nope, just the writing grandmother. "You are?" I asked like an awkward teenager. "Why?"

Smiling warmly, she urged me to sit down so we could talk about the first chapter of my manuscript. "Because I wondered who could write such a lovely story," she began.

I think my index fingers may have gone to my ears to clean them. "Could you repeat that?"

She laughed. "I love your story. I love your protagonist, Sarah. I'd follow her anywhere, and I would love to see where her story leads."

I could not breathe. "You love Sarah?" I echoed.

She nodded.

"You mean you actually like my story? My writing?" I looked at my clothes and around the room. I had to make sure I wasn't back in my fantasy. I wasn't wearing PJs and I wasn't at home, so it had to be real.

"In fact, just today the conference organizers asked each of the editors and agents to choose our favorite manuscript from all those we have evaluated, and I chose yours," she said. "Tonight a grand prize will be awarded to the best of the best. I hope yours wins. It deserves to."

Okay, deal or no deal, I cried. I just sat there like a loony old woman and cried. Somehow I knew that the Muse up above didn't mind at all.

~Susan Mayer Davis

What Makes Me Whole

I became a writer in the deep woods of Vermont. Every afternoon, I climbed down the school bus steps and began the mile-long walk up Kimball Farm Road. As the noise of the school day drained away, stories filled my head. I plugged my nose walking by the Spakmans' farm to mask the smell of cow manure and wet hay. Dragging my feet, I passed the Mahers' house with the barn where I once dared my friend Alex to eat horse food. I hoped for Pepperidge Farm cookies if "Grannie" Maher heard my dragging feet. If she didn't offer me a ride home, I'd continue my walk and go back to the story in my head. My stories were about popular girls with names like Elizabeth or Jessica, who had long hair and rode horses. As my house appeared through the birch trees, I'd linger outside on the porch. Swinging my legs over the edge of the deck, I wove my tales until I was ready to let go.

When my sister started first grade she joined me on my walk, and my storytelling afternoons were over.

"What do you do if you have to go to the bathroom?" she asked. Then, "Why aren't you talking to me?"

I tried to ignore her, but it was useless; she continued to pester me with her inquisitive chatter. I sighed heavily and explained about the stories in my head, and she demanded to hear them. I didn't want to share, but she persisted. So I tried to explain what Elizabeth looked like, the color and length of her hair, and how she wore it in a ponytail when she rode horses, but the words got caught in my throat. I couldn't do the voices, and Elizabeth sounded dull out loud. Erin began kicking the rocks in the road and saying she was hungry.

The next day when we got off the bus, the stories didn't come. I tried to think about where I'd left off, but drew a blank. My breathing felt tight, and I blamed my sister; she'd ruined everything! I walked quickly home and picked up a notebook and pen, because I didn't want to forget. I sat down at my desk and started to write.

When I wasn't making up stories, I was reading them. Mom read books to my sister and me every night. Even though we didn't have much money, going to the library made me feel rich. I read both to escape and to understand my world. Stumbling through major life events, I clutched a book in front of me like a map. Judy Blume helped me feel connected in my adolescence. I felt closer to Margaret in *Are You There God? It's Me, Margaret* than I did to Tiffany or Lisa at school. In college I read *The Awakening* and suddenly saw my mother as a woman. Kate Chopin allowed me to make room in my heart to forgive my parents' divorce.

While vacationing on an island off the coast of Maine, I found a blue hardback journal and wrote with colored pens, filling the heavy, cream-colored pages with my words. After I'd filled the last page, I searched in bookstores for another journal with the same heavy pages and dreamed about returning to the island to write my stories.

Soon journals in a rainbow of colors and textures filled my nightstand, spilling out onto the floor: brown leather, pastel stripes, spiral black-and-white, written in pencil and sometimes even crayon, whatever was at hand. Bored and restless, I wrote on my lunch break at my desk in the shoe stockroom. The journals were a reminder of where I'd been, who I was, and where I hoped to go.

After meeting my future husband, I sat down and wrote him a letter, taking that first step forward. We began a long-distance love affair, and for our first

Christmas together I gave him a scrapbook of our letters and pictures. When he opened it, he cried, and
I knew then the power of our words. As we planned
our wedding, I picked up my pen again and wrote a
letter to our guests, asking them to put their thoughts
on marriage into words. I gingerly opened each envelope and discovered stories of intimacy and struggles.
Their words reassured me and helped prepare me for
the next step.

While expecting our first child, I walked every
morning along a wooded path that used to be a rail-
road track. I let the quiet of the morning surround
me as I tried to sort out the worries in my head. *Will
he be healthy? Will I be able to nurse? How can I possibly go back to work at a meaningless job?* I walked
slowly, thinking of my baby boy in a day care or at
home with a nanny, someone else's arms holding
this child who moved inside yet was still unknown
to me. *Wouldn't it be great if I could stay home with my
baby and call myself a writer? Wouldn't it be great to be
paid to write?* I began to walk faster. A story began
to take shape. I hurried home and grabbed a pen
from the kitchen drawer, still sweating as I wrote,
smearing the words with my scribbling hand. When
I stopped to take a breath, the story was no longer
about Elizabeth. The story was about me and what
I wanted as a wife, a mother, and a writer.

As the mother of two young boys, I am a writer, but my storytelling time is limited. During my toddler's nap, I make the beds and put away the dishes. I try to spend time with my older son doing puzzles or drawing. By the time the boys are in bed each night, I collapse onto the couch with a magazine or a book, and I read someone else's story. I write when I can. The boys are my muses, my inspiration, and my roadblocks to writing. I am greedy with my laptop and secretive with my stories. While the boys jump from the couch to the chair, I write about taking them to church and Will's questions about God. With Play-Doh spread across the table, Will cutting and Miles eating dough, I write about trying to relax. While the boys watch cartoons, I write about the commercials for McDonald's, and my struggle to keep our family healthy. I sit at the dining table with my laptop and gaze out the window. Will asks for a snack while I struggle for the right word, and Miles pulls on my arm as I type. I stare into the past, and as the words begin to flow, I breathe easier.

Writing reminds me that there is a world outside our home; it awakens me and fills me up. When I feel defeated by the laundry and monotony of our days, I return to the stories in my head. When I am sleep-deprived and irritable, I reach for my notebook. My stories have changed from popular girls and their horses to motherhood and marriage. Instead of walking up Kimball Farm Road, I run on the old wooded path. As my mind empties of the *Thomas the Tank Engine* theme song, my stories return. I am a girl again, focused on the contents in my head and blind to the world around me.

So when I ask the boys to let me work, when I shush them and ask them to play in the back, I hope they will understand that I have dreams of my own. I hope that when they listen to my stories, they will hear the confidence in my voice. When they point to the magazine rack outside the bookstore that has my story, I hope they see my feet planted firmly beside them. I hope one day they'll know that writing makes me a better mother. It is what makes me whole.

~*Amy S. Mercer*

The Truth about Lies

One of my favorite writers, Anne Lamott, came to visit. She didn't come to see me personally; she came to Dutton's bookstore down the street.

Last year, when I launched my new career as a writer, I'd sent around announcements, little blue cards that contained my contact information and e-mail. I addressed one of them to Anne Lamott in care of her publisher and stuck it in the mailbox. *What the heck?* I thought. *Maybe she'll check out my Web site.* I never heard back. But now here she was—giving a reading in my hometown—and I couldn't wait to meet her, even if it meant driving down Wilshire Boulevard in the pouring rain.

I brought my husband, Ron, to the event. He shook out the umbrella as we stepped inside the bookstore.

"See, babe?" I said, looking around. "You're not the only guy here."

There were at least two others. Never mind that Anne Lamott later introduced the first one as family. The second guy tapped Anne Lamott's arm as she walked by.

"Can you sign my copy of your book?" he asked, holding it up.

Anne Lamott told the man she had arthritis. Then she made an announcement to the entire crowd: "If you want me to sign your books, you can write any introduction you want, and I'll write my name underneath it. But if I start inscribing more than my name, my hand will be sore tomorrow."

She perched on a table in front of the crowd. She wore a pink sweater and jeans, a pair of funky black shoes, and a necklace with a moon and a star. Her spirally dreadlocks flopped around (who would've thought dreadlocks could look darling on anybody?). In between readings, she answered questions.

"How do I write autobiography without hurting friends and family?" a woman from the audience asked.

I wonder the same thing. Writing personal essays, memoir, and even my blog, I wonder that a lot. At first, Anne Lamott gave a standard answer: change names and identifying characteristics; there are lawyers who worry about those details; blah, blah, blah. But then she stopped and shifted positions.

"Keep writing," she said. "Keep telling the truth. There's so little of that going on in the world." She looked around. "Right?"

The audience nodded.

"As women, we're taught to keep quiet," she continued. "We're taught to believe it's wrong to talk about certain issues. But it's such a relief when someone tells the truth."

It is. Telling the truth is one of the best, but most difficult, parts about writing. In daily conversation, I tend to let white lies fall from my lips. More lies swarm my brain and try to convince me of some reality that, deep down, I know isn't true. When I put pen to paper, I can explore those lies. I can ask myself, Why did I tell Ron I spent $60 on my yellow sweater when I'd spent $110? Why did I tell myself I ate three chocolate chip cookies when I ate five? It's easy to see my lies when I write, the black-and-white statements staring directly at me from the page. Inspecting those lies eventually helps me gain insights about my life and who I am as a person. And that's what writing is meant to do.

Later, at the book signing table, I handed Anne Lamott my copy of her book, *Plan B: Further Thoughts* on *Faith*. She read the introduction that I'd scribbled inside: "Keep writing. Keep telling the truth. There's so little of that going on."

"A quote from you," I said.

"So true," she nodded her head.

Anne Lamott signed her name and put a little heart by it. Then she closed the book and looked up at me. "I really like your wr—"

Time stopped.

In that instant—before she finished the word—time stopped. Here's what raced through my brain: *She's going to say "writing." Wow! She's going to say she really likes my writing. She did receive my announcement—maybe she's even read my blog. Wow!*

Anne Lamott finished the word: "—aincoat."

I looked down at my jacket, its print of colorful flowers.

"Thanks," I said, giving my coat a little tug.

Ron was waiting for me between two aisles of books.

"Anne Lamott likes my raincoat," I told him as I spun around, displaying it.

"I heard," he said.

I stopped spinning and began frowning as we walked to the door.

"I thought she was going to say she liked my writing," I sulked.

Outside, Ron opened the umbrella and waited for me to step underneath it. We headed down the street to Xi'an restaurant.

"She'll say that to you one day," Ron said.

I looked at him with hope. "You think so?" I asked.

"Yep," he said, "I do."

If Ron's statement was a lie, it was a beautiful lie. But I hope he was telling the truth.

~Jenny Rough

Tell Your Story in the Next
Cup of Comfort®

We hope you have enjoyed *A Cup of Comfort*® *for Writers* and that you will share it with all the special people in your life.

You won't want to miss our next heartwarming volumes, *A Cup of Comfort*® *for Single Mothers*, *A Cup of Comfort*® *for Horse Lovers*, and *A Cup of Comfort*® *for Cat Lovers*. Look for these new books in your favorite bookstores soon!

We're brewing up lots of other *Cup of Comfort*® books, each filled to the brim with true stories that will touch your heart and soothe your soul. We would love to include one of your stories in an upcoming edition of *A Cup of Comfort*®.

Do you have a powerful story about an experience that dramatically changed or enhanced your life? A compelling story that can stir our emotions, make us think, and bring us hope? An inspiring story that reveals lessons of humility within a vividly told tale? Tell us your story!

Each *Cup of Comfort*® contributor will receive a monetary fee, author credit, and a complimentary copy of the book. Just e-mail your submission of 1,000 to 2,000 words (one story per e-mail; no attachments, please) to *cupofcomfort@adamsmedia .com*. Or, if e-mail is unavailable to you, send it to:

A Cup of Comfort
Adams Media
57 Littlefield Street
Avon, MA 02322

You can submit as many stories as you'd like, for whichever volumes you'd like. Make sure to include your name, address, and other contact information and to indicate for which volume you'd like to be considered. We also welcome your suggestions for new *Cup of Comfort*® themes.

For more information, please visit our Web site: *www.cupofcomfort.com*. We look forward to sharing many more soothing *Cups of Comfort*® with you!

Contributors

Judy L. Adourian ("The Write Mother") works as a writing coach through her company, Writeyes. Her writing is featured regularly online at *Inkwell Newswatch* and in *NEWN* magazine, for which she is the executive editor. She is also the Rhode Island regional representative for the International Women's Writing Guild. This is her fourth *Cup of Comfort*® publication.

Sally Bellerose ("The Zen of Rejection") is a writer who lives and works in Northampton, Massachusetts. Her novel, *The Girls Club*, was a finalist for the Bellwether Prize, the James Jones First Novel Fellowship, and the Thomas Wolfe Fiction Prize. It won first place and a fellowship from Writers at Work and a National Endowment for the Arts Creative Writing Fellowship in Prose. Excerpts from the book have been published in *The Sun*, *The Best of Writers at Work*, and *Quarterly West*. The manuscript, as a whole, alas, remains unpublished.

Kathy Briccetti ("The Drowning Girl") holds an M.F.A. from Stonecoast. Her writing has been published in national magazines and newspapers as well as in anthologies and on public radio. She is at work on a memoir about three generations of adoption and absent fathers and is represented by the Randi Murray Literary Agency.

Sage Cohen ("Flow") lives in Portland, Oregon, where she is a freelance writer and editor. Sage serves as managing editor for *Writers on the Rise* and writes a monthly column for *Black Lamb*. Her writing has been published in journals, including *Poetry Flash*, *Oregon Literary Review*, and *San Francisco Reader*. She recently won first prize in the Ghost Road poetry contest.

Harriet Cooper ("Charity Begins at My Keyboard") is a Toronto, Canada, humorist and essayist. When not playing cards or knocking on doors, she writes articles on health, fitness, nutrition, family, relationships, and anything else that tickles her funny bone. Her work has appeared in numerous magazines, newspapers, anthologies, radio, and on a coffee can.

Amy Rose Davis ("Heritage of Words") and her husband, Bryce, live in Gresham, Oregon, with their four children. Amy works as a freelance business copywriter and ghostwriter, and her work has appeared in *A Cup of Comfort® for Mothers-to-Be*, *Northwest Construction* magazine, and the *Oregon Humane Society* magazine.

Susan Mayer Davis ("The Deal") is a writer/editor for a nonprofit organization. At home, she divides her leisure time among writing, reading, and oil painting. An award-winning fiction writer, she is currently working on her first novel. Susan lives in Snellville, Georgia, with her family and their rescued lab, Abby.

Marla Doherty ("Potty Talk") coordinates the Northern California Authors' Fair and enjoys writing articles, poetry, fiction, and creative nonfiction, including stories in previous *Cup of Comfort®* volumes (*Mothers & Daughters* and *Women in Love*.) Her creed in writing and in life: live, love, laugh, and embrace failure.

Stacey Donovan ("Thomas Wolfe Wasn't Kidding") is the author of *Dive*, *Who I Am Keeps Happening*, and *The Last Four-Letter Word*, the coauthor of the four-book fictional series *Zalman King's Red Shoe Diaries*, and the nonfiction work *Your Fate Is in Your Hands*. A ghostwriter and editor of several other works of fiction and nonfiction, she lives in Amagansett, New York.

Peggy Duffy ("Learning to Listen") lives in Northern Virginia. She is the sales manager for a real estate firm and a freelance writer. Her essays and short stories have appeared in regional and national magazines, newspapers, literary journals, online publications, and anthologies, including two previous *Cup of Comfort®* volumes. Her children's book, *The Little Sister I Almost Had*, is still looking for a publisher.

Ellen Dworsky ("Nonfiction Nightmares") is a California native who has lived in Israel, Italy, Brazil, and the even-more-foreign land of Minnesota. She's still not sure how she wound up in Minneapolis, where she finished her B.A. and went on to get her M.F.A. in creative nonfiction at the University of Minnesota. Her work has appeared in many magazines and literary journals.

Pat Gallant ("On Unconditional Love and Rejection Slips") is a native New Yorker and freelance writer. Her literary nonfiction has appeared in numerous publications, including the *Saturday Evening Post, Writer's Digest, A Cup of Comfort® for Christmas, Family Gatherings*, and *The Simple Pleasures of Friendship*. She is a four-time winner of the New Century Writer's Award and has been a finalist for the William Faulkner Literary Competition and the PEN Syndicated Fiction Project.

Kathleen Gerard ("The Day I Turned Scarlett") lives in New Jersey. Her work has been widely published and anthologized. Several of her plays have been staged and performed regionally and off-Broadway in New York City.

Denise R. Graham ("The Big Hiatus") is the author of *Eye of Fortune* and *Curse of the Lost Grove*, Young Reader fantasy/mysteries. Her stories have appeared in the *Dragons of Magic* and *Monsters of Magic* anthologies and *Woman's World* magazine. She lives near St. Louis, Missouri, with her husband, the inimitable Ron Morris. She loves NaNoWriMo and Writers Under the Arch.

Christina Hamlett ("Memoirs of a Shiksa") is an award-winning author and screenplay consultant whose credits include twenty-five books, 121 plays and musicals, four optioned feature films, and hundreds of articles and interviews in publications throughout the world. A former actress and theater director, Christina resides with her husband, Mark Webb, in Pasadena, California.

Jana Harris ("Bountiful Hunger") has published two novels, many short stories and essays, and eight books of poetry, the most recent being *We Never Speak of It, Idaho-Wyoming Poems 1889–1890*. She is the founding editor of the online poetry journal *Switched-on Gutenberg* and teaches poetry online at the University of Washington. She and her husband raise horses in the Cascade foothills.

Jan Henrikson ("Jump") coaches writers and plays with words in Tucson, Arizona. She is the editor of *Eat by Choice, Not by Habit*, by Sylvia Haskvitz. Her essays, articles, and interviews have appeared in everything from WritersDigest.com to *Chicken Soup for the Dieter's Soul*.

Roberta Beach Jacobson ("Confessing in 5,000 Steps") is a kid at heart. At twenty-one, she left Chicagoland to explore Europe. After two decades of traveling, she settled on the isolated Greek island of Kárpathos, where she spins words and feeds cats.

Meridian James ("Me, an Artist") writes for her living and lives for her writing in the San Francisco Bay area. In addition to creating materials for high-tech clients, she writes personal essays, memoir, and short fiction.

Diana Jordan ("The Queen of Procrastination") is a broadcast journalist, news anchor/reporter, and talk show host for radio stations in Portland, Oregon, and Los Angeles, California. A nationally known author and celebrity interviewer on *AP*

Radio Network, BarnesandNoble.com, and *TV Book Reviewer,* her author interviews and book reviews also appear regularly in national magazines and books. She has two sons, two cats, and a dog.

Lauren Kessler ("Wasting Time") is the author of six narrative nonfiction books, including her most recent, *Dancing with Rose: Finding Life in the Land of Alzheimer's* (Viking). Her work has appeared in the *New York Times Sunday* magazine, the *Los Angeles Times Sunday* magazine, and Salon.com. She lives in Eugene, Oregon, where she directs the graduate program in literary nonfiction at the University of Oregon.

Brenda Kezar ("Lament of the Aspiring Writer") is a writer and home-schooling mom living in North Dakota. She and her husband have two daughters and share their home with two dogs, multiple cats, and an assortment of small animals. Between hairballs, she writes every chance she gets.

Mimi Greenwood Knight ("Something to Say") is a freelance writer, living in what's left of south Louisiana with her husband, David, four kids, four dogs, four cats, and one knuckle-headed bird. Her work has appeared in *Parents* magazine, *Working Mother, American Baby, Today's Christian Woman, Christian Parenting Today, Campus Life,* and a spattering of anthologies.

Stephanie Losee ("We Are Mortified by You") is a journalist who lives in San Francisco with her husband and three daughters. Her work has appeared in publications that include *Fortune,* the *Los Angeles Times,* the *New York Post, Child, The Huffington Post,* and the *San Francisco Chronicle Magazine.* Her new book, written with Helaine Olen, is *Office Mate: The Employee Handbook for Finding—and Managing—Romance on the Job.*

Kathryn Magendie ("To Begin") is a western North Carolina writer who often contemplates the glow of Old Moon over the Smokies. She is in the query process of her first novel, has published her short stories and essays here and there, and is an editor at *The Rose & Thorn* literary e-zine.

Allison Maher ("About My Promise to My Mother") lives on a fruit farm in Nova Scotia, Canada, with her two children and husband, David Bowlby. She writes articles for newspapers and magazines, and in the spring of 2006 she published her first novel, with two more expected to follow.

Lori Maliszewski ("Groupie") spent more than twenty years in high-tech marketing before retiring and becoming a writer. She's finishing her memoir, *Cancer, A Love Story*, and her story "Time" was published in *How to Leave a Place*, an anthology of short memoirs edited by Ariel Gore. She and her husband live in Portland, Oregon.

Phyllis Ann Mannan ("The Echolalia of Literature"), a former high school teacher, lives with her husband in Portland, Oregon. They plan to retire soon to Manzanita, on the Oregon Coast. Another of her stories appears in *A Cup of Comfort®️ for Parents of Children with Autism*.

Chris J. Markham ("The Writer Who Couldn't Read") is a New Jersey–based freelance photographer and writer whose work has appeared in numerous publications, including the *Iconoclast, Modern Short Stories, Fiction Writers Monthly*, and *Grit*. He is the author of *Mississippi Odyssey*, a journal of his adventures hitchhiking boat rides down the Mississippi River.

Marian Van Eyk McCain ("The Baptism"), a retired psychotherapist, writes on many subjects, from psychology to organic gardening. She is the author of three books: *Transformation through Menopause; Elderwoman: Reap the Wisdom, Feel the Power, Embrace the Joy*; and *The Lilypad List: 7 Steps to the Simple Life*. She lives in England.

Lorri McDole ("Time Enough") is a writer who lives in a suburb of Seattle with her husband and two children. She has worked as a technical and marketing writer for various

Northwest companies and has published in *Pacific Northwest, Common Ground, Brain/Child,* and *Urban Spaghetti.*

Karen McQuestion ("Of Rewrites and Restitution") resides in Hartland, Wisconsin, with her husband and three children. Her writing has appeared in *Newsweek,* the *Chicago Tribune,* the *Christian Science Monitor,* the *Denver Post,* the *Wisconsin Academy Review,* and other publications. In addition, she was awarded a winter/spring 2003 Ragdale Foundation residency for fiction.

Amy S. Mercer ("What Makes Me Whole") is a freelance writer who lives in Charleston, South Carolina, with her husband and two young sons. Her personal essays have been published in *Skirt!* magazine, *Literary Mama, Byline* magazine, and *Mamazine.* Her sons are both an inspiration and a roadblock to the writing that makes her feel whole.

Camille Moffatt ("Why Write?") lives in the middle of the woods on the side of an ancient mountain. From there, she writes, watches the seasons pass, and walks beneath wise old trees with her tiny granddaughter, Naomi.

Amy A. Mullis ("The Greatest Gig on Earth") lives with husband, Bill, and Sons One and Two in upstate South Carolina. She would run away and join the circus, but her Ho Hos habit keeps her from fitting into the clown car. A church secretary, she contributed to *Stories of Strength,* an anthology published to benefit survivors of Hurricane Katrina.

Paula Munier ("Falling in Love Again") is a veteran writer and editor who acquires books for a nonfiction publisher by day and writes mysteries by night. The author of *Emerald's Desire* and *On Being Blonde,* she lives on the South Shore of Boston with her family.

Becky Mushko ("Out of the Fog"), a retired English teacher residing in Penhook, Virginia, writes the Peevish Advice column for the *Smith Mountain Eagle.* She was a nominee for the 1997 Pushcart Prize and the 1996 Worst Western winner in the infamous Bulwer-Lytton contest. Her stories have been published in THEMA, Blue Ridge Traditions, and Virginia Adversaria, and she has self-published four books.

Ava Pennington ("The Inklets") is a freelance writer who resides in Stuart, Florida, with her husband, Russ. With an M.B.A. from St. John's University and a Certificate from Moody Bible Institute, the former human resources director now spends her time teaching Bible studies, writing, and doing public speaking. Her publishing credits include magazine articles and short stories.

Felice Prager ("Writing without Pizza") is a professional freelance writer from Scottsdale, Arizona, with local, national, and international credits. In addition to writing, she is a multisensory educational therapist, which is a fancy way of saying she works with children and adults who have moderate to severe learning disabilities.

Kathryn Presley ("Out of Dry Ground") is a retired English professor who lives in Bryan, Texas, with her husband of fifty-four years, Roy Presley. She has published numerous poems, short stories, essays, and devotionals in anthologies (including A Cup of Comfort®), professional journals, and national magazines. She teaches Bible studies and has been a conference speaker for decades.

Carol McAdoo Rehme ("Of Trifles and Truffles"), a freelance author and editor based in Loveland, Colorado, publishes prolifically in the inspirational market. As the founding director of Vintage Voices, Inc., a grassroots nonprofit that provides interactive arts programs in nursing-care facilities, Carol gleans captivating stories and life lessons from the frail elderly.

Lisa Romeo ("I Remember Anna") is an M.F.A. student of creative nonfiction at the University of Southern Maine's Stonecoast Program. Her work has appeared in dozens of periodicals, including The Victorian Reader, O The Oprah Magazine, L'Anne Hippique International, and the anthology Special

Gifts: Women Write on the Happiness, Heartache, and Hope in Raising a Special Needs Child. She lives with her husband and two children in Cedar Grove, New Jersey.

Jenny Rough ("The Truth about Lies") is a freelancer writer who splits her time between the congested city of Washington, D.C., and the wild, free land of southwest Colorado. She's working on a book of essays. When Jenny's not planted in front of her laptop, she's hanging out with her husband, Ron.

Cynthia Ruchti ("Reading by Flashlight, Writing by Heart") writes and produces "The Heartbeat of the Home" radio broadcast. Cynthia's articles and devotionals appear in numerous magazines and newspapers, including a column for *Wisconsin Christian News* and a humor column for *American Christian Fiction Writer's Aficionado* e-zine. A devoted wife, mother, and delightfully indulgent grandmother, she makes her home in Wisconsin.

Valerie Schultz ("Raw Material") is a freelance writer in Tehachapi, California. Her work has appeared in the *Los Angeles Times*, the *Chicago Tribune*, and numerous Catholic and parenting publications. She is a weekly columnist for the *Bakersfield Californian* and a monthly columnist for *Liguorian*. She and her husband, Randy, have four daughters, ages twenty-three, twenty-two, eighteen, and sixteen.

Alaina Smith ("Addiction") is a contributor to multiple volumes of two anthology series, *Chocolate for Women* and *A Cup of Comfort®*. Having completed a novel and many short stories, she's on the lookout for dealers to feed her publication addiction. She lives near Portland, Oregon, with her husband, Frank.

Valetta Smith ("The Only Cure for the No-News Blues") is a full-time writer living in Lebanon, Oregon. She has had short stories and essays published in several different magazines. While the first book of her mystery series is making the rounds in search of a publisher, she is working on the second one.

Cassie Premo Steele ("Hummingbird's Journey") is an award-winning poet and writer. She is the author of the books *Moon Days*, *We Heal from Memory*, and *Ruin* as well as hundreds of essays, poems, and short stories on the themes of healing women's bodies and spirits. She lives in Columbia, South Carolina, where she teaches women's studies at the University of South Carolina as well as "writing with the body" classes at AMSA Studios.

Alarie Tennille ("Talking on Paper"), a graduate of the University of Virginia, inherited her love of storytelling from her Southern parents. A writer for Hallmark Cards, Alarie lives in Kansas City, Missouri, with her husband, Chris, and three cats. Her poems have appeared in *Kansas City Voices, I-70 Review*, and the *Kansas City Star*.

Samantha Ducloux Waltz ("A New Point of View") and her husband, Ray, live in Portland, Oregon. Her current writing passion is the personal essay. Her work can be seen in the *Christian Science Monitor* and a number of anthologies, including several in the *Cup of Comfort®* series. She has also published fiction and nonfiction under the name Samellyn Wood.

George Weinstein ("23½ Love Letters") lives with his wife, Kate, and their two furry children, Ruby Slippers and Angie Anne, in Roswell, Georgia. He writes novels, short stories, and essays, and he is president of the Atlanta Writers Club.

Gila Zalon ("The Voice in My Head") lives and works with her attorney husband in their newly purchased fixer-upper New Jersey home. Amid the clutter, they periodically host their three children and two grandchildren and sundry other relatives and friends. In this exciting environment, Gila is in pre-production on a full-length film she wrote, and she is rewriting her second feature-length screenplay.

About the Editor

Colleen Sell is the editor of nineteen volumes of the *Cup of Comfort*® book series. She has been a book author, editor, and ghostwriter as well as a magazine editor, journalist, technical writer, and copywriter. She and her husband, T. N. Trudeau, share a big old farmhouse on a forty-acre pioneer homestead in the Pacific Northwest, which they are slowly turning into an organic lavender, blueberry, holly, and pumpkin farm.

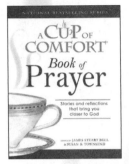

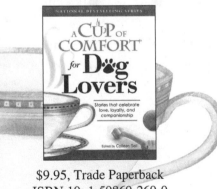